TODD KELLY'S
Orchids at Palm Court

Recipes from the Hilton Cincinnati Netherland Plaza
with Courtney Tsitouris

9 8 7 6 5 4 3 2 1

Printed in South Korea

ISBN 978-1-4507-9336-0

Recipes by
Todd Kelly

Cowritten by
Courtney Tsitouris

Photography by
Rasul K Welch

Design and Layout by
Kelly Pennington

Edited by
Stephanie Meinberg

Published by Black Tie Press,
A Division of Black Tie Productions, Inc.
P. O. Box 14527
Cincinnati, OH 45250

www.blacktieinc.com
www.cincinnatinetherlandplaza.hilton.com
www.orchidsatpalmcourt.com

CONTENTS

A HISTORY OF DISTINCTION

The Hilton Cincinnati Netherland Plaza is a true French Art Deco masterpiece and a National Historic Landmark. Opened in 1931, the hotel was an integral part of the first multi-use complex in the United States. Described as a "city within a city," it featured an office tower, hotel, fully automated garage, shopping complex, and restaurants. Novel in 1929, the concept would grow in popularity when Rockefeller Center was later constructed in New York City.

When the Netherland Plaza opened, critics raved that it "challenged the splendor of King Solomon's Temple." Every detail was artfully refined—from the rare Brazilian rosewood in the main lobby, Palm Court, and mezzanine to the exquisite frescoes, ceiling murals, German silver, and delicate floral motifs. Even the hotel's ballrooms were grandly appointed—including the renowned Hall of Mirrors modeled after the Palace of Versailles in Paris, the Continental Room with striking floor-to-ceiling windows, and the Pavillion Ballroom where Doris Day made her professional singing debut. Perfect for meetings and banquets, these spaces have been historically preserved to showcase their original beauty.

From the beginning of its history, food and dining were integral to the Netherland Plaza concept. Eleven kitchens and seven restaurants spanned the space—including the Frontier Room, the Restaurant Continentale, the Arcadia Tea Room, the Coffee Shop, the Rotisserie Grill, the Luncheonette, and the Pavillion Caprice. In the early 1980s, during one of several renovations and upgrades, the hotel introduced Orchids at Palm Court. Now the Netherland Plaza's flagship restaurant, Orchids has become a destination in and of itself, nationally celebrated for its high level of service and cuisine.

PIONEERS OF INNOVATION

Walter W. Ahlschlager
Designer
Previous works include the Peabody Hotel in Memphis and the Hotel InterContinental in Chicago

Colonel William A. Starrett
Builder
Previous projects include the Lincoln Memorial and the Empire State Building

---

■ 5

FORWARD

The Hilton Cincinnati Netherland Plaza has been an icon for Cincinnati and Cincinnatians since opening its doors in January of 1931.

Welcoming world travelers to the Queen City of the West, the hotel's lavish food and beverage venues have always been highly regarded by our guests. Chef Kelly has continued this long tradition, and in the process, established Orchids at Palm Court as a locally and nationally regarded restaurant. His remarkable abilities to utilize classical preparation techniques to deliver imaginative and beautifully harmonized food have rightly earned him the many accolades he has received—including the American Culinary Federation's highest award, 2011 Chef of the Year.

Equally impressive are his substantial skills in developing the culinary and service staffs at the hotel, both demanding and encouraging the best from the staff in each area. This approach has energized our work throughout the hotel, including our remarkable private event spaces.

The Netherland Plaza has been a locally owned institution since its inception, and continues to be to this day. We are especially grateful to the owners for their support of Chef Kelly's work, and their vision, passion, and commitment to the continued future success of the hotel. They are remarkable stewards of this great institution, and for this and much more, we thank them.

This book is the work of many hands, and we are grateful to them all, especially Megan Ketover and Bob Louis. On behalf of the entire staff of the Netherland Plaza, thank you for your patronage of our hotel.

Michel A. Sheer

Michel A. Sheer, Managing Director

ACKNOWLEDGMENTS

First, my thanks to Emily for her support—whether I'm getting up in the middle of the night to scribble down ideas or working long hours on a holiday. Being a chef is full of challenges, but being a chef's wife is the hardest job of all. You have handled the demands of my career with patience and grace.

And of course, love and thanks to my daughters, Madeline and Megan, whose smiles and laughter have enriched my life. I've made a career out of creating lavish meals, but nothing is better than pizza night with you.

To my mother, Kathy, thank you for keeping me grounded and for teaching me the values and work ethic that have made my career possible. And much gratitude to my brother, Brad, for getting me started in this career, for supporting me during the hardest of times, and for being a constant source of inspiration.

Thank you to the Hilton Cincinnati Netherland Plaza team for making this book a reality. Especially the ownership group and Managing Director Michel Sheer, whose belief in me has allowed me to paint the canvas. Michel is a tremendous mentor and leader—and his tenacity and passion for achieving excellence are contagious.

To Charles Redmond, Maître D', thank you for staying with me all these years and for sharing the same desire for distinction. Your sophisticated palate and ability to run a seamless and beautiful dining room have made Orchids at Palm Court what it is today. Jenny Filipiski, Manager, The Bar at Palm Court, thank you for your tireless work ethic and commitment to running one of the region's most celebrated destination bars.

Finally, my deepest thanks to the culinary staff and the food and beverage team at the Netherland Plaza, especially Pastry Chef Megan Ketover, without whom we could not receive such high praise, loyal following, and distinctive awards. You are the true leaders in the culinary world.

Gary Davis, Banquet Chef
Chris Stephens, Sous-Chef
Brendan Haren, Sous-Chef
Wesley Furomoto, Garde Manger Chef
Jackie Djordjevic, Banquet Sous-Chef
Derek Bush
Helen Cain
Walter Coman
Patrick Gedroic
Tom Groves
Tim Ingram
Natasha Miller
Eric Munchel
Aaron Neiman
Dana Perryman
Mirko Ravlic
Allison Schweizer
Steve Simms
Eli Sitterding
Nathaniel Turnbolt
Max Wagner
Nick Wise
Katie Wulf
George Zappas
Valerie Rodriguez,
*   Stewarding Manager*
Jorge Martinez, Director of Banquets
Ned Softic,
*   Assistant Director of Banquets*
Barbara Sharp, Restaurant Manager
Ken Mendelsohn, Restaurant Manager
Kathleen Murphy,
*   Room Service Supervisor*

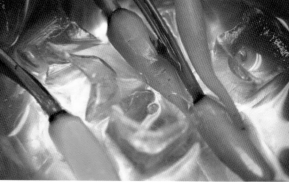

Stories from a lifetime of food

Great cooking is about more than knife skills—and it's about more than timing and technique. Great cooks know this, which is why we dedicate so much of our lives to traveling, eating, observing, working for little pay in hot, crammed spaces, and learning from anyone who will spare us a second.

Truly great cooking is about bringing your life to the table in whatever way you can find to articulate. And so, as you thumb through the recipes in this book, know that they're the product of the experiences I've had, the chances I've taken, and the people who have invested their time in me. You can cook these recipes exactly, or you can use them as a foundation to incorporate your own story.

Of course, I didn't understand all of this until I was older—and I was either very foolish or very wise to believe that my life would bring me here—in the center of so much opportunity. At Orchids at Palm Court in the Hilton Cincinnati Netherland Plaza, I have the resources to make the kind of food that young chefs dream about—and the kind of support and teamwork that great food requires.

But my journey has been anything but straightforward—and in many ways, it began long before I knew I was on my way.

THE ROAD TO ORCHIDS AT PALM COURT

I was twelve when my family moved from New York to Mauritius, an island off the coast of Africa in the Indian Ocean. Our new address meant having to adapt to an unfamiliar diet: exotic spices, powdered milk, very little beef. There were other peculiarities, too—the kind that opened my eyes to food and forced me to see it in a new way. Bread was delivered daily by moped. Local fisherman walked through backyards to sell fresh catch.

When we returned to the states from Mauritius, I had developed a fascination with food—which was heightened by the fact that my older brother, Brad, went away to culinary school. When I turned 17, I took a job in the hotel kitchen where he worked as a prep cook. Uncertain if I wanted to spend my life cooking—but determined to prove that I was as fast and smart as him—I developed a relentless work ethic. While my friends were off at football games and parties, I peeled potatoes until my hands cramped. Even more than math and science, my education was about learning kitchen basics: what a hotel pan was, how to dice an onion, and how to use the food processor without jamming the lid.

After a few years of grunt work, I decided to move to a higher-end restaurant in town. When I got there, the cooks were running around the kitchen at warp speed: baking bread, butchering fish, and making pastries. I was amazed with the production—the symphony of movement. Despite getting bumped and nudged and feeling mostly in the way, I managed to learn a lot about fine cuisine—from how to make stocks and soups from scratch to how to butcher fresh fish. So, when my brother urged me to go work alongside him at a restaurant called Doneckers, I felt ready and up to the challenge.

Of course, Brad had much more experience than me, and at Doneckers, he drove me crazy—constantly ordering me to line up my spices and to collect my ingredients before every new task. I didn't know it at the time, but

in an industry that requires painstaking preparation and relentless organization, he was teaching me how to survive.

As my curiosity in culinary matters increased, so too did my yearning to see more of the country. Having a few friends in Pittsburgh was enough reason for me to pack my bags and take a job at a small Italian restaurant in the city. The kitchen immediately seduced me—and I learned a lot about handcrafted pastas, earthy sauces, and fresh pizza crust. But even more than technique, I learned about the pace, the heat, and the lifestyle of a cook. And I became convinced that the more kitchens I could experience and the more chefs I could work for, the more valuable I would become. When given the chance to move to an upscale restaurant downtown, I didn't hesitate.

It was a place with extraordinary city views and an even more extraordinary clientele: business people, athletes, theater-goers. The chef was a known talent with a weekly rotating menu, a cutting-edge concept at the time. I was committed to learning everything I could from him. For over a year, I worked hard on the line—soaking up every

bit of technique as possible, demonstrating as much focus and enthusiasm as I could, and eventually earning the position of Sous-Chef.

Around this time, I was seeing a girl named Emily who was also in the restaurant industry. When compelled once again to experience another piece of the American landscape, Emily and I decided to do it together—and we moved to Charlotte, North Carolina. I got a job at a prestigious country club working for a chef who was not only on the culinary Olympic team, but was preparing for his Certified Master Chef Exam.

As my mentor for a number of years, he helped me advance from prep cook to Garde Manger Chef to Banquet Chef to the restaurant's highest position, Chef de Cuisine. During the process, I learned how to prepare pâtés and terrines, smoke meat, perform advanced charcuterie work, and plan, organize, and execute multicourse meals for hundreds of people at a time. At the end of my tenure, I had worked from the ground up, grunted it out in nearly every station, and climbed my way to the top. For a kid from New York, once unsure of his future, I had finally discovered something I was passionate about. And I knew that it was time to take my career to the next level.

COMING INTO MY OWN

I was twenty-five, and I had just been offered my first position as Executive Chef at a restaurant on the west coast in a trendy San Francisco neighborhood called North Beach. Emily and I had no choice but to pack up our things again and sell everything we could to make the move.

Over the next year, I took regular trips to ethnic areas of the city and experienced as many different cuisines as possible—eating fresh crab at the Wharf, going to the farmers market at the Embarcadero, and taking trips to Chinatown and Japantown. For the first time, I was working directly with farmers and fishermen to find the freshest, highest-quality ingredients I could get my hands on.

Despite the thrill, Emily and I had agreed that our time in San Francisco was temporary. And I knew that before we left, I had to experience working in a high-profile restaurant kitchen. That's when I made the move to one of America's most iconic restaurants: Drew Nieporent's Rubicon. Known for its high level of California-French cuisine, Rubicon only employed the highest caliber of cooks. Each one was more passionate and devoted to their craft than the next, and the competition was fierce. Under Chef Dennis Leary, the standards were higher than ever.

Every day, we cooked from scratch. Ingredients leftover from the previous day were only to be used in the staff meal. After having advanced from line cook to Sous-Chef, much of this responsibility fell on me. I had to manage the purchases so that we had just enough ingredients for service and no more. It was a maddening process and required a fastidious attention to detail—one that often left me questioning the very practice itself.

Even so, I eventually found myself managing purchasing with a similar philosophy. And in time, it became apparent that Leary's eccentric devotion to fresh ingredients had actually become my own.

A RETURN TO THE BEGINNING

Emily and I returned to North Carolina in 2002 to get married. Around this time, a local restaurateur offered

me what seemed like a once-in-a-lifetime opportunity: a chance to open and run a brand-new restaurant. I eagerly accepted the job—and for the next year, I worked diligently, focused on every detail of the restaurant's success.

But something under the surface was brewing. I started to wonder if all of my experience at independent restaurants was stifling my ability to make a contribution on a much bigger level. In the hotel industry, I would have more ability to demonstrate all I had learned over the years—from the bar snacks to the banquet spreads to the elegant, multicourse meals.

My entrée back to the hotel industry was as Chef de Cuisine of a new hotel restaurant in Charlotte—a food and beverage operation that buzzed from morning to night. I loved the wealth of resources and the organized chaos: the banquet, the bar, the restaurant. And with thirty cooks under my supervision, I learned quickly how to manage people, and how to get them to work hard for me and for our diners.

In the kitchen, I applied everything I had ever learned about work ethic, organization, and technique. And it seemed to be paying off. The restaurant began winning awards. The press started writing glowing reviews. Professionally, I felt like I had found my place—and back at home, I knew that it was time for Emily and me to build a house and a family.

LUCK, DESTINY, OR BOTH?

In 2006, I received a phone call from a recruiter about a job at the Hilton Cincinnati Netherland Plaza. Having little knowledge of the city and unprepared to uproot my wife and daughter, I declined the offer. Even so, Michel Sheer, the hotel's Managing Director, was persistent—and eventually flew me out to see the restaurant.

A series of surprising incidents followed—both lucky and fateful—and they would forever change the course of my career. I walked into Orchids at Palm Court for the first time and was completely in awe of the grandiose architecture, the golden embellishments, and the mural-painted ceilings. I learned that joining the team would mean an opportunity to orchestrate all the details—from selecting the china and the linens, to the suppliers and the ingredients, to the menu and the wine list. With a solid management team already in place, I would have a wealth of resources and amenities at my disposal.

The restaurant seemed like a blank canvas—simply in need of some paint. So, after seriously weighing the options with my family, we packed our bags one last time and moved to Cincinnati.

Located in the heart of Ohio's agricultural belt—and with access to some of the best ingredients in the world—the menu at Orchids at Palm Court today is fueled by the kind of food I've wanted to make all my life. It's about drawing from techniques I've learned along the way and pushing them in new and inventive ways. And it's about bringing my stories to the plate—all the way from the fresh pasta in Pittsburgh to the Dungeness crab in San

Francisco. The result is even more meaningful than I could have imagined. Not just because of our loyal diners, but because I've become part of a community that I can finally call home.

After almost twenty years in the business, I have developed a rhythm and a balance in cooking—whether I'm building a new dish around a special ingredient or introducing a new twist on an old favorite. It's a constantly evolving style that inspires me on the farm, at the market, and in the Orchids kitchen. And one that, I hope, will inspire you as you cook from this collection of some of the most delicious dishes we've made over the last five years.

STARTERS

There's nothing better than the creamy mouthfeel of oyster velouté—though a spoonful of cauliflower custard with smoked bacon is an extraordinary way to begin a meal. Such is the power of starters and small bites. They don't rely on a combination of meat, starch, and vegetables because diners are more willing to take chances. Experiment. Discover. This translates to an exciting, heightened sense of creativity in the kitchen. Attention is focused solely on delivering supremely focused, impactful flavor. And in this way, we raise the bar for each course that follows.

Saffron Cauliflower Custard with House-Smoked Bacon, Domestic Caviar, and Crème Fraîche

10 pieces smoked bacon

20 eggs, reserving 6 yolks

1 1/2 tablespoons vegetable oil

2 ounces chopped onion

1/2 sliced garlic clove, peeled

5 inches chopped celery rib

1/2 chopped shallot

1/2 chopped leek

1 head chopped cauliflower

1 cup Chardonnay

2 tablespoons saffron

2 3/4 cups heavy cream

Kosher salt and white pepper, to taste

1/2 cup crème fraîche (pg 168)

1/2 ounce Big Fish Farms paddlefish roe

1 tablespoon micro chives

Preheat the oven to 350 degrees.

Place the bacon between two sheet pans lined with parchment paper. Bake for 15 minutes or until cooked through.

Meanwhile, use an egg topper to remove the tops of 20 eggs. Reserve 6 yolks for the cauliflower custard and save the rest for another use. (Make sure to remove the thin membrane inside the shells under running water.) Place the shells back in their cartons and set aside.

In a large pot, add the vegetable oil and sweat the onions, garlic, celery, shallots, and leeks over medium heat until cooked through, about 5 minutes. Add the cauliflower and cook until soft, about 5 minutes more. Pour in the wine and saffron, and reduce by half. Add half the heavy cream, bring to a simmer, and remove from heat.

In a mixing bowl, combine the 6 reserved egg yolks with the rest of the cream and whisk. Slowly temper this mixture into the pot of cauliflower—stirring constantly so that the eggs do not scramble. Season with salt and white pepper.

Place the cauliflower mixture in a blender and purée until smooth. Strain through a chinois and discard the solids.

This elaborate version of a custard-filled egg makes a fantastic impression at the start of a meal. Each eggshell is filled with a saffron-spiked custard and topped with a single slice of smoked bacon. Drizzled with caviar, the dish becomes a rich luxury that's hard to forget.

TO COMPLETE: Lower the oven to 275 degrees. Place the egg cartons in a baking dish, and fill the dish halfway with water. Fill each eggshell with the cauliflower purée, then bake covered with foil until the eggs are soft set, approximately 20 minutes.

TO SERVE: Garnish each egg with a small dollop of crème fraîche, a teaspoon of caviar, a half slice of bacon, and micro chives.

Makes 20 eggs

Floating Mozzarella with 3-Hour Tomatoes, Roasted Fennel, Lavash, and Tomato Water Gelée

TOMATO WATER GELÉE

2 cups tomato water (pg 164)

1/2 teaspoon kosher salt

2 gelatin sheets, soaked
in cold water to soften

3-HOUR TOMATOES

1 pint cherry tomatoes

2 cups extra virgin olive oil

3 garlic cloves, peeled

Sea salt and black pepper, to taste

ROASTED FENNEL

2 tablespoons unsalted butter

1 julienned fennel bulb

Kosher salt and white pepper, to taste

SHALLOT LAVASH

2 1/2 cups all-purpose flour

1 teaspoon sugar

1 teaspoon kosher salt

2/3 cup water

2 egg whites

2 tablespoons unsalted butter, melted

2 tablespoons chopped shallots

1 tablespoon sea salt

FOR THE TOMATO WATER GELÉE: In a sauce pot, simmer the tomato water and salt over medium heat until reduced to 1 cup. Remove the pot from the heat and add the bloomed gelatin. Whisk until dissolved, and then strain through a chinois. Pour the liquid into 6 serving dishes and let set in the refrigerator.

FOR THE 3-HOUR TOMATOES: Cut a shallow "x" in the bottom of each cherry tomato and blanch for 10 seconds in a large pot of boiling water. Remove the tomatoes with a slotted spoon and drop them into an ice bath to stop further cooking. Peel the tomatoes and set aside.

Fill an immersion circulator or a large, heavy pot with 2 cups of olive oil. Heat the oil to 125 degrees, and cook the tomatoes and garlic cloves gently for 3 hours. Reserve warm or refrigerate until needed.

FOR THE FENNEL: Preheat the oven to 350 degrees.

Melt the butter in a large, oven-ready skillet and add the fennel. Cook for 3-4 minutes over medium heat until some of the moisture from the fennel has been released. Place the skillet in the oven for 10 minutes or until the fennel has caramelized. Season to taste with salt and white pepper.

FOR THE LAVASH: Increase the oven to 400 degrees.

In a large bowl, mix the flour, sugar, and salt until well incorporated. Add the water, the first egg white, and the melted butter. Stir with a spoon until the mixture turns into a stiff dough. Knead the dough for 5 minutes, and then roll it into a paper-thin sheet with a rolling pin. Brush the top of the dough with the remaining egg white. Sprinkle the surface with shallots and a pinch of sea salt.

Cut the dough into triangles so that the longest edge is approximately 3 inches long. Place the triangles on an ungreased baking sheet and bake for 10-12 minutes or until light brown and crispy.

Recipe and ingredients continued on the page 20.

Caprese salad is all about freshness. I serve mine with thickened tomato water, which is simply a purée of tomatoes and salt strained and clarified overnight. The dish has a pure, concentrated flavor that I love.

MOZZARELLA

4 ounces kosher salt
1/2 gallon water
1 pound mozzarella curd

1/4 cup wild arugula
1 tablespoon lemon vinaigrette (pg 164)
Kosher salt, to taste
1 tablespoon extra virgin olive oil
Sea salt, to taste

FOR THE MOZZARELLA BALLOON: Salt a large pot of simmering water. Dice the cheese curd into 1-inch pieces. Place the curd in a mixing bowl and ladle the saltwater over the top, just to cover. Let the curd steep for 2 minutes, then drain. Repeat this process two more times—draining the water and steeping the curd in saltwater.

On the third steep, gently pull the curd out of the water with a wooden spoon and stretch. Suspend the cheese using two wooden spoons, allowing gravity to stretch the cheese as it falls back into the water. Repeat this process until the cheese is smooth.

Place a small portion of cheese in your hands and roll into a ball. Use a sugar pump to gently blow air into the cheese, forming a balloon. Pinch the cheese off at the end to seal. Repeat until you have 6 balloons. (The balloons will stay inflated for 2-3 minutes.)

TO COMPLETE: Toss the arugula with the lemon vinaigrette and salt. Reheat the tomatoes in a warm oven and toss with sea salt and black pepper.

TO SERVE: Place the fennel and tomatoes in the center of the prepared serving dishes. Top with lavash, wild arugula, and a mozzarella balloon. Drizzle with olive oil and a pinch of sea salt.

Makes 6 servings

Recipe Variation

A quicker but equally impressive way to make this dish is to omit the fennel and lavash and serve the mozzarella without being inflated. At Orchids at Palm Court, I serve this version as an amuse-bouche with 1-hour tomatoes and a gently fried basil leaf.

1-HOUR TOMATOES

1 pint cherry tomatoes
2 cups extra virgin olive oil
3 garlic cloves, peeled
Sea salt and black pepper, to taste

6 basil leaves, lightly fried
in vegetable oil

FOR THE ONE-HOUR TOMATOES: Preheat the oven to 250 degrees.

Cut a shallow "x" in the bottom of each cherry tomato and blanch for 10 seconds in a large pot of boiling water. Remove the tomatoes with a slotted spoon and drop them into an ice bath. Once cool, peel the tomatoes and toss them with the olive oil and garlic cloves. Place them in a small, oven-ready pan and bake covered in foil for 1 hour. Season with sea salt and black pepper. Place the tomatoes and mozzarella in the center of the prepared serving dishes. Garnish with a fried basil leaf.

Crispy Artisanal Feta Cheese with Katafi, Heirloom Eggplant, Harissa, and Herbed Crème Fraîche

FETA

8-ounce block feta cheese
All-purpose flour, for dredging
1/4 cup egg wash
1 box katafi dough
1/4 cup chopped oregano
Vegetable oil, for frying
Kosher salt and black pepper, to taste

EGGPLANT

2 eggplants
Vegetable oil, for frying
2 tablespoons extra virgin olive oil
1 tablespoon sliced garlic cloves
1 tablespoon chopped shallots
1/4 cup harissa sauce
4 roasted red peppers
(pg 169), puréed
1/4 cup chopped parsley
Kosher salt and black pepper, to taste

HERBED CRÈME FRAÎCHE

4 ounces crème fraîche (pg 168)
1 1/2 tablespoons chopped oregano
1/2 lemon, juiced
1/2 teaspoon extra virgin olive oil
1/2 teaspoon minced shallot
1/2 teaspoon minced garlic
Kosher salt and black pepper, to taste

2 tablespoons parsley oil
(pg 169), in a squeeze bottle

FOR THE FETA: Slice the feta cheese into 4 rectangular blocks. Roll each block of cheese first in a shallow bowl of flour and then coat in egg wash.

Unroll the katafi dough, working quickly so that it does not dry out. Divide the dough into strands long enough to wrap around a block of cheese with a little overlap, and then sprinkle with oregano. Place the cheese in the center of the dough and wrap tightly around all sides. Repeat for all blocks of cheese and set aside.

FOR THE EGGPLANT: Remove the skin from the eggplant and discard. Dice the eggplant into 1-inch cubes.

Pour vegetable oil into a deep-fryer or a large, heavy pot and heat to 350 degrees. Fry the eggplant in batches for 3 minutes or until golden brown. Remove with a slotted spoon, drain on a paper towel, and reserve.

In a pan with 2 tablespoons of olive oil, sauté the garlic and shallots over medium heat. Cook the vegetables until fragrant and tender, mixing constantly to avoid any browning. Pour in the harissa sauce and red pepper purée, and stir until well incorporated. Add the reserved eggplant, and braise until mixture is the consistency of a thick stew. Fold in the parsley, and season with salt and pepper.

FOR THE HERBED CRÈME FRAÎCHE: Mix all the ingredients together and season with salt and pepper.

TO COMPLETE: Pour vegetable oil into a deep-fryer or a large, heavy pot and heat to 350 degrees. Fry the cheese in batches for 3 minutes or until golden brown. Remove the cheese and drain on a paper towel. Season with salt and pepper.

TO SERVE: In the center of each serving plate, pour the parsley oil around the interior of a 3-inch ring mold, then stack the eggplant inside about 2 inches high, and remove the mold. Add a feta cheese stick and a streak of herbed crème fraîche.

Makes 4 servings

Eggplant is a classic ingredient in braised vegetarian stews, and it was my inspiration for this dish, which has a deep and hearty, almost jammy consistency. After frying the eggplant, I sauté it in a spicy North African hot sauce called harissa. Topped with feta cheese wrapped in crispy katafi dough, it's an incredibly delicious way to begin any meal.

Honeycrisp Apples with Foie Gras Torchon, 8 Brix Verjus, Tatsoi, and Za'atar Croutons

FOIE GRAS TORCHON

1 pound foie gras

1/2 gallon milk

3 tablespoons kosher salt

1/4 teaspoon sugar

1/2 teaspoon tinted cure mix

1/4 cup brandy

APPLES

2 Honeycrisp apples

1 quart Pinot Noir

1/2 cup sugar

1 star anise

2 tablespoons mustard seeds

8 BRIX VERJUS GEL

3 3/4 cups water

5 ounces sugar

1 tablespoon kosher salt

1 tablespoon lemon zest

3/4 ounce agar powder

1 1/8 cups 8 Brix Verjus

ZA'ATAR CROUTONS

1 baguette

1 tablespoon extra virgin olive oil

2 tablespoons za'atar

Kosher salt and black pepper, to taste

1/2 cup micro tatsoi

1 tablespoon lemon vinaigrette (pg 164)

4 drops 50-year-old balsamic vinegar

FOR THE FOIE GRAS: Soak the foie gras in milk overnight. Remove from the milk and bring to room temperature.

Separate the lobes, making sure to remove any veins and bruises. (Foie gras is malleable, so it will go back together if you need to pull it completely apart.) Using your fingers, press the foie gras into a 1-inch-thick layer.

Combine the salt, sugar, and tinted cure mix. Season the foie gras with this mixture and drizzle the brandy on top. Refrigerate in a plastic-wrapped container for 24 hours.

Bring the foie gras to room temperature. Spread out over a layer of cheese-cloth and roll carefully into a tight cylinder. Roll the cheesecloth again in a kitchen towel and tie the ends securely in a knot.

Bring a large pot of water to a simmer. Remove the towel and gently poach the foie gras for 2 minutes. Blot it dry and then hang by a string in the refrigerator overnight.

My favorite way to eat foie gras is cold—after it's been tightly rolled, poached, and cooled. Served this way and paired with sweet Honeycrisp apples, it's the perfect fall indulgence. Make sure to begin preparations at least three days in advance so that the flavors in the foie gras have enough time to develop properly.

FOR THE APPLES: Peel the apples and slice them horizontally so that they form 3-inch-thick rings. Place them in a large mixing bowl and set aside.

In a large pot, bring the remaining ingredients to a boil. Pour the boiling liquid over the apples and cover with plastic wrap. Refrigerate overnight.

Recipe continued on the page 26.

FOR THE VERJUS GEL: In a sauce pot, bring the water, sugar, salt, and lemon zest to a boil. Remove the pot from the heat and let the mixture steep for 20 minutes. Strain through a chinois and return the liquid to the pot.

Add the agar powder and bring to a boil. After 2 minutes, strain the liquid through a chinois onto a sheet pan lined with plastic wrap. Place the sheet pan in the refrigerator for 2 hours or until the gel is set.

Pour the mixture into a blender, add the verjus, and blend on high for 1 minute. Reserve in the refrigerator until needed.

FOR THE CROUTONS: Preheat the oven to 350 degrees.

Cut the bread into several paper-thin slices. Toss the bread with olive oil, za'atar, salt, and pepper. Lay the pieces out on a sheet pan and bake for 5 minutes or until golden and crispy.

TO COMPLETE: Toss the tatsoi in 1 tablespoon of lemon vinaigrette and set aside.

Slice the cold foie gras the same width as the apple slices. Remove the apple cores with a 2-inch ring cutter. Use the same ring cutter to punch out a series of circles from the foie gras slices.

TO SERVE: Center an apple ring on each plate and place a circle of foie gras inside. Top with a crouton—making sure to keep half the apple and foie gras exposed. Drag a tablespoon of the verjus from one side of the plate to the other. Garnish with tatsoi and 1 drop of 50-year-old balsamic vinegar.

Makes 4 servings

Duet of Tuna with Lychees, Pickled Shiitake Mushrooms, Sprouts, and Satsuma Mandarin Orange Miso Aioli

MARINATED TUNA

1 cup white miso

1/2 cup soy sauce

1 tablespoon lime zest

2 tablespoons truffle juice

1/2 cup truffle oil

10 limes, juiced

10 roasted garlic cloves (pg 167)

5 ounces #1 sushi-grade tuna fillet

1 tablespoon vegetable oil

Kosher salt and black pepper, to taste

TUNA SPRING ROLL

8 ounces diced #1 sushi-grade tuna

2 julienned radishes

1 tablespoon chopped cilantro

1/2 minced jalapeño, seeds removed

1/2 tablespoon chopped ginger

1/2 tablespoon chopped shallots

1 tablespoon coriander oil (pg 165)

1 tablespoon lemon vinaigrette (pg 164)

Kosher salt and black pepper, to taste

Vegetable oil, for frying

2 spring roll wrappers

2 egg whites, beaten for egg wash

5 tablespoons sesame seeds

FOR THE MARINATED TUNA: Mix the first 7 ingredients together in a blender. Refrigerate the tuna with the marinade in an airtight container for at least 3 hours.

This dual presentation of tuna is served on a Himalayan salt block. Not only is it an impressive presentation, the salt actually seasons the fish as it's being eaten. Even if you don't have a salt block, the seared loin fanned around a crispy tuna spring roll makes a statement, especially when topped with my orange miso aioli.

FOR THE SPRING ROLL: Toss the first 8 ingredients together in a bowl and season with salt and pepper. Refrigerate until ready to serve.

Pour vegetable oil into a deep-fryer or a large, heavy pot and heat to 350 degrees.

Cut a 4-inch prepared spring roll wrapper in half lengthwise. Wrap it around a 1-inch cannoli tube, making sure the ends overlap. Brush both ends with egg wash to ensure they stick together.

Brush the entire surface of the spring roll wrapper with egg wash and sprinkle with 1 tablespoon of sesame seeds. Let the spring roll dry for at least 3 minutes and then plunge into the fryer for 2 minutes or until golden brown.

Drain the spring roll on a paper towel and gently remove the cannoli tube. Repeat this process until you have 4 fried cylinders.

Recipe and ingredients continued on page 29.

PICKLED MUSHROOMS

1 cup water

1/2 cup rice wine vinegar

1/2 cup sugar

2 teaspoons kosher salt

1 teaspoon mustard seeds

1 star anise

1 teaspoon black peppercorns

2 garlic cloves, peeled

1 teaspoon chopped ginger

1/2 minced jalapeño, seeds removed

8 ounces julienned shiitake mushrooms

MUSHROOM AND LYCHEE SALAD

2 ounces daikon sprouts

15 fresh lychees, peeled and
seeds removed

Kosher salt and black pepper, to taste

4 tablespoons Satsuma mandarin
orange miso aioli (pg 168)

Micro greens or herb shoots

FOR THE PICKLED MUSHROOMS: Combine the first 10 ingredients in a medium sauce pot and boil until the salt and sugar have dissolved. Allow the mixture to cool to room temperature. Repeat this process once more—bringing the mixture to a boil and then cooling to room temperature. Strain the liquid through a chinois.

Place the mushrooms in a medium saucepan and pour the liquid over the top. Bring the mixture to a boil again and cover with plastic wrap. Set aside until ready to serve or refrigerate for up to 4 hours.

FOR THE MUSHROOM AND LYCHEE SALAD: In a mixing bowl, combine the daikon sprouts, lychees (with accumulated juices), and pickled shiitake mushrooms. Season with salt and pepper.

TO COMPLETE: Stuff the tossed tuna tartare into the prepared spring roll tubes, being careful not to let them crack. Dip the exposed ends in the remaining sesame seeds.

Drizzle 1 tablespoon of vegetable oil in a hot pan and sear the marinated tuna on all sides until caramelized. Slice the tuna into 1/2-inch-thick pieces and season with salt and pepper.

TO SERVE: Place the mushroom salad in the center of a salt block or a large serving platter. Fan the seared tuna around the salad. Place a spring roll on top of the salad, and garnish with Satsuma mandarin orange miso aioli and micro greens or herb shoots.

Makes 4 servings

Maine Lobster Salad with "Crispy" Poached Egg, Parsley, and Domestic Caviar Cream

CRISPY EGG

2 eggs
1 sheet bric dough
1 cup all-purpose flour
2 eggs, beaten for egg wash
Vegetable oil, for frying
Kosher salt and black pepper, to taste

CAVIAR CREAM

1 cup heavy cream
1 tablespoon red wine vinegar
1 tablespoon Big Fish Farms caviar
Kosher salt and black pepper, to taste

PARSLEY PURÉE

1 cup chopped parsley
1 tablespoon water
Kosher salt and black pepper, to taste

LOBSTER SALAD

1 pound Maine lobster
1/2 cup crème fraîche (pg 168)
1 tablespoon chopped chives
1 tablespoon chopped shallots
1 tablespoon lemon vinaigrette (pg 164)
Kosher salt and black pepper, to taste

FOR THE CRISPY EGG: To poach the eggs, bring a small pot of water to a simmer. Carefully break the eggs into the pot. Cook until the egg whites are set, 1 or 2 minutes. Remove the eggs with a slotted spoon and place them in an ice bath to stop the cooking process. When cool, remove the eggs and pat dry with a paper towel.

Roll the bric dough into a long cigar shape, and then chiffonade. Prepare the breading station. Place the flour, egg wash, and bric dough into three separate shallow bowls. Coat the poached eggs in flour first, shaking off the excess. Transfer to the egg wash and coat evenly. Finish by rolling in bric dough.

Pour vegetable oil into a deep-fryer or a large, heavy pot and heat to 350 degrees. Fry the eggs for 1 minute or until golden brown. Remove the eggs from the oil and drain on a paper towel. Season with salt and pepper and reserve warm.

FOR THE CAVIAR CREAM: Combine all the ingredients in a small bowl and set aside. Be careful not to overmix the cream.

FOR THE PARSLEY PURÉE: Purée the parsley in a blender—adding only enough water to turn the blade. Blend on high for 1 minute, and season with salt and pepper.

FOR THE LOBSTER SALAD: Fill a large pot with water and season generously with salt. Bring to a boil and stir until the salt is completely dissolved.

Place the lobster in a separate large pot and pour the boiling liquid over the top. Off the heat, let the lobster cook in the hot water for 7 minutes. Strain and let the lobster cool. Remove the lobster meat from its shell. Dice into bite-size pieces and toss with the crème fraîche, chives, shallots, and lemon vinaigrette. Season to taste with salt and pepper.

TO SERVE: Using a 3-inch ring mold, place the lobster salad in the center of each plate, about 1 inch high. Garnish with a crispy fried egg and dots of the parsley purée. Drizzle the dish with caviar cream and serve immediately.

Makes 2 servings

Here, diced lobster becomes an elegant pedestal for a crispy poached egg—wrapped in bric dough and flash-fried in hot oil. I finish the dish with a touch of caviar cream—poured tableside for an over-the-top, dramatic presentation.

Tuna Tartare with Watermelon Radishes, Cucumber Water, and Lemon Oil

CUCUMBER WATER

2 cucumbers

2 tablespoons kosher salt

POTATO TUILE

1 large Idaho potato

3 tablespoons unsalted butter

1 teaspoon saffron

3 egg whites

1/4 teaspoon ground ginger

Kosher salt and black pepper, to taste

2 tablespoons pink peppercorns

TUNA TARTARE

12 ounces diced #1 sushi-grade tuna

3 julienned radishes

2 tablespoons chopped cilantro

1 minced jalapeño, seeds removed

1 tablespoon chopped ginger

1 tablespoon chopped shallots

2 tablespoons coriander oil
(pg 165)

3 tablespoons lemon vinaigrette
(pg 164)

Kosher salt and black pepper, to taste

1 ounce micro cilantro

1 watermelon radish, sliced on
a rotating mandolin*

1 tablespoon lemon oil

FOR CUCUMBER WATER: Roughly chop the cucumbers and place them in a blender with the salt. Purée until well incorporated and strain through a chinois or a chinois lined with cheesecloth. Reserve chilled.

FOR POTATO TUILE: Preheat the oven to 350 degrees.

Bake the potato for 1 hour or until tender and easily pierced with a fork. Peel the potato while still warm and pass through a tamis.

Melt the butter and saffron in a small sauté pan. Pour into a bowl with the potato, egg whites, ginger, salt, and pepper. Blend until ingredients are well incorporated.

Create a stencil by cutting a series of four 2x4-inch rectangles out of a thin sheet of plastic. Line the template over a silpat and spread the potatoes out within the rectangle spaces. Carefully remove the template and bake the potatoes for 10 minutes. Once crispy, remove the potatoes from the oven and sprinkle with ground pink peppercorns.

I keep coming back to this dish because of one key component: coriander oil. It works really well with the tartare, which fuses Asian-style ingredients and French-inspired preparation. Cucumber water, which is simply a purée of cucumbers and salt, gives the dish a clean, refreshing finish and a vibrant presentation.

TO COMPLETE: Gently toss the tuna tartare ingredients in a mixing bowl and season with salt and pepper.

TO SERVE: Using a small square ring mold, place the tuna tartare mixture in the center of 4 shallow bowls. Pour the cucumber water around the mold. Garnish with a potato tuile, micro cilantro, and watermelon radishes. Add a few drops of lemon oil to the cucumber water and serve cold.

Makes 4 servings

*A rotating mandolin is similar to a standard Japanese mandolin, but is connected to a crank and produces curly-shaped strings of vegetables.

Dean Family Farm Porchetta with Preserved Lemons, Radishes, and Arugula

1 Red Wattle pig's head
2 lemons, zested
3/4 cup chopped parsley
1/2 cup chopped oregano
1 1/2 teaspoons tinted cure mix
1/4 cup kosher salt
1 tablespoon black pepper

2 julienned preserved lemons (pg 166)
2 fuyu persimmons, cut into wedges
1 cup wild arugula
4 radishes, thinly sliced on a mandolin
1 cup extra virgin olive oil
Cracked black pepper, to taste

Under cold running water, clean the pig's head—washing away the dirt and making sure to rinse the inside of the ears. Once clean and dry, remove the pig's hair with a disposable razor and a blowtorch. Give the head a final rinse and pat dry with a towel.

Starting at the bottom of the pig's jaw, use a sharp knife to cut away the meat from the bone—being especially careful around the eyes and ears—and avoiding rips or tears in the skin. Remove the tongue and place the thickest part into the snout. Make sure to keep the snout intact as you work.

In a bowl, mix together the lemon zest, parsley, oregano, tinted cure mix, salt, and pepper. Season both sides of the meat with this mixture, and place in the refrigerator for 1 hour.

Roll the meat in plastic wrap, returning the head to its original shape. Secure the plastic wrap tightly. Fill a large stockpot with water and heat to 180 degrees. Place the meat in the water and poach until its internal temperature reaches 150 degrees. Remove the head and reserve in the refrigerator for 2 days to develop its flavor.

We're fortunate to get heirloom heritage pigs from the Dean Family Farm in Georgetown, Ohio, and we love to utilize the entire animal—whether we're making lardo, bacon, or prosciutto. Here, we roll, poach, and cure the meat from the pig's head to create paper-thin slices of porchetta, which have a sensuous, melt-in-your mouth quality that I love.

TO SERVE: Remove the meat from the plastic wrap and slice into thin pieces on a meat slicer. Garnish with preserved lemons, persimmons, arugula, and radishes. Drizzle the plate with olive oil and season with cracked black pepper.

Makes 7 servings

Shrimp Cavatelli with Tomato Concassé, Braised Fennel, and Clam Nage

PASTA

2 cups all-purpose flour

1 egg, plus 8 egg yolks

2 teaspoons extra virgin olive oil

1 tablespoon kosher salt

1 tablespoon milk

CLAM NAGE

1 medium chopped leek

1 medium chopped celery rib

2 minced shallots

1/4 cup unsalted butter

1 cup dry vermouth

1 cup Chardonnay

5 pounds littleneck clams

4 parsley stems

10 peppercorns

1 bay leaf

1 quart water

FENNEL

1 julienned fennel

2 tablespoons unsalted butter

1 cup Chardonnay

3 thyme sprigs

FOR THE PASTA: Combine all the ingredients in a stand-up mixer fitted with a hook attachment. Beat on medium speed for 10 minutes. Knead for 15 minutes and refrigerate the dough for 1 hour.

Divide the dough into 10 equal sections. Roll each section into a thin rope about 1/2 inch in diameter, then cut each one into 1-1/2-inch pieces.

Using your thumb, gently press down in the center of each piece of dough, causing it to roll over on itself. With the palm of your hand, rock the dough from side to side—creating a small pouch with a hollow center.

Cook the pasta in generously salted water for 3 minutes or until tender. Cool the pasta in an ice bath, strain, and reserve.

This dish will shake your expectations of shrimp pasta—from the light mouthfeel of the handcrafted cavatelli to the focused flavors of clam nage. Learning to shape the pasta properly will take practice—but be patient. The hollow centers hold the sauce and deliver an unexpected punch of flavor.

FOR THE CLAM NAGE: In a large sauce pot, sweat the leeks, celery, and shallots in butter over low heat. Continue to cook for 30 minutes, stirring occasionally so that the vegetables do not brown. When all the liquid is released and the vegetables are very tender, add the vermouth and wine. Reduce the liquid by half. Add the clams and cover, cooking for an additional 4 to 5 minutes or until the shells open.

Remove the clams with a slotted spoon and cool slightly so that you can pull the meat from their shells. Add the shells to the pot, reserving the meat for another use. Add the parsley, peppercorns, bay leaf, and water. Simmer over low heat until reduced by half. Strain and discard the solids, reserving the clam broth.

Recipe and ingredients continued on page 38.

GARLIC CHIPS

6 sliced garlic cloves, peeled

3 cups milk

Vegetable oil, for frying

Kosher salt, to taste

24 16/20 shrimp, peeled and cut in half from head to tail

2 tablespoons clarified butter

3 cups spinach

1/2 cup tomato concassé (pg 164)

3 tablespoons unsalted butter

2 tablespoons extra virgin olive oil

FOR THE FENNEL: Sweat the fennel over low heat in butter for 10 minutes or until tender and translucent. Add the wine and thyme sprigs, and cover with a lid. Simmer the mixture gently for 15 minutes.

FOR THE GARLIC CHIPS: Place the garlic slices in a sauce pot with 1 cup of milk. Bring the mixture to a boil. Discard the milk and rinse the garlic slices under cold running water. Repeat this process 2 more times. Use a paper towel to soak up the excess moisture.

Fill a large, heavy pot or a deep-fryer with vegetable oil and heat to 325 degrees. Fry the garlic slices until golden brown and crispy, about 3 minutes. Remove the garlic and drain on a paper towel. Season with salt immediately.

TO COMPLETE: Sauté the shrimp in clarified butter for 1 minute or until almost all the way cooked through. Add the clam nage and fennel, and continue to simmer until the shrimp is completely cooked, about 1 minute more. Stir in the spinach and tomato concassé. Add the cavatelli and stir until warmed through. Swirl in 3 tablespoons of butter to finish.

TO SERVE: Pour the shrimp cavatelli in the serving bowls. Garnish with garlic chips and a drizzle of olive oil.

Makes 6 servings, with leftover pasta

Veal Sweetbreads with Celery Salad, Haricots Verts, Shiitake Mushrooms, and Smoked Paprika Vinaigrette

SWEETBREADS

1 pound veal sweetbreads

1 quart milk

2 quarts chicken stock (pg 166)

2 bay leaves

2 tablespoons peppercorns

1 medium diced carrot

1/2 diced onion

1 medium diced celery rib

Kosher salt and black pepper, to taste

All-purpose flour, for dredging

2 tablespoons clarified butter

1/4 cup red wine vinegar

SMOKED PAPRIKA VINAIGRETTE

1 minced shallot

1 teaspoon unsalted butter

2 tablespoons smoked paprika

1 cup sherry vinegar

1 1/2 cups grape seed oil

1 teaspoon Dijon mustard

CELERY SALAD

2 celery ribs

1/4 cup buttermilk

2 tablespoons red wine vinegar

Kosher salt and black pepper, to taste

FOR THE SWEETBREADS: Soak the sweetbreads in milk overnight. Discard the milk and set aside.

In a stockpot, bring the chicken stock, bay leaves, peppercorns, carrots, onions, and celery to a simmer. Add the sweetbreads and gently poach for 15 minutes.

Discard the poaching liquid and place the sweetbreads in the refrigerator between 2 large pans with at least 3 pounds of cans on top. Let them compress overnight so that any excess moisture is removed. (Skipping this step will result in an undesirable, spongy texture.)

Remove the outer membranes from the sweetbreads and cut them into 3-inch pieces. Set aside.

FOR THE VINAIGRETTE: In a small saucepan, sweat the shallots in butter and cook over low heat until translucent. Add the paprika and continue to cook until fragrant, about 1 minute more. Add the sherry vinegar and simmer until reduced by half. Remove the pot from the heat, and add the grape seed oil and Dijon mustard. Set the vinaigrette aside until ready to serve.

Refined dishes are often inspired by simple comfort foods. This crispy sweetbreads recipe is my take on classic chicken wings with a few enhancements. Instead of traditional bar condiments, like hot sauce and blue cheese, I drizzle smoked paprika vinaigrette over the top of a buttermilk celery salad.

FOR THE CELERY SALAD: Peel and cut the celery on a bias into 2-inch pieces. Blanch the pieces in generously salted water for 20 seconds and then plunge in an ice bath to stop further cooking.

In a mixing bowl, toss the celery with the buttermilk and red wine vinegar. Season to taste with salt and pepper.

Recipe and ingredients continued on page 41.

MUSHROOMS

1 tablespoon clarified butter

12 sliced shiitake mushrooms

2 tablespoons minced shallots

1 tablespoon chopped garlic

1 teaspoon chopped thyme

1 tablespoon unsalted butter

HARICOTS VERTS

20 haricots verts

Kosher salt and black pepper, to taste

FRISÉE SALAD

1/2 cup frisée

1 tablespoon lemon vinaigrette
(pg 164)

1 tablespoon chopped chives

Kosher salt and black pepper, to taste

12 purple potato chips (pg 168)

FOR THE MUSHROOMS: In a medium sauté pan, heat 1 tablespoon of clarified butter on high and add the mushrooms. When the edges start to brown, flip them and cook for another minute. Add the shallots, garlic, thyme, and unsalted butter. Remove the pan from heat and set aside.

FOR THE HARICOTS VERTS: In a pot of boiling salted water, cook the haricots verts for 30 seconds. Strain the water, and season to taste with salt and pepper.

FOR THE FRISÉE SALAD: Toss the frisée with lemon vinaigrette, chives, salt, and pepper. Set aside.

TO COMPLETE: Season the sweetbreads with salt and pepper. Dredge them in flour, shaking off the excess. Over medium heat, cook the sweetbreads in 2 tablespoons of clarified butter until golden brown on all sides, about 3 minutes.

Pour out the excess butter and deglaze the pan with red wine vinegar. Continue to cook until the liquid is completely evaporated. Season to taste with salt and pepper.

TO SERVE: Place celery salad in the middle of a serving platter. Garnish with an arrangement of mushrooms and haricots verts. Place the sweetbreads on top, followed by frisée, purple potato chips, and 2 tablespoons of paprika vinaigrette.

Makes 4 servings

Smoked Salmon with Red Onion Marmalade, Crème Fraîche, and Potato Crisp

SMOKED SALMON

7 ounces kosher salt

4 ounces sugar

2 teaspoons onion powder

3/4 teaspoon cloves

3/4 teaspoon ground bay leaves

1 tablespoon Chinese five-spice

1/8 teaspoon tinted cure mix

1 3-pound side of salmon

MARMALADE

2 tablespoons extra virgin olive oil

6 sliced red onions

1 tablespoon chopped ginger

1 tablespoon chopped garlic

1 1/2 cups red wine vinegar

1 1/2 cups Pinot Noir

1 cup sugar

POTATO CRISP

2 baking potatoes, peeled
and sliced on a rotating mandolin*

2 cups cornstarch

Vegetable oil, for frying

Kosher salt, to taste

1/4 cup crème fraîche (pg 168)

1 tablespoon chives

FOR THE SMOKED SALMON: Combine the first 7 ingredients in a mixing bowl.

Cut a piece of cheesecloth so that it doubles the length of a baking sheet. Lay out flat on the baking sheet, and sprinkle with a thin layer of seasoning. Place the salmon on top, skin-side-up, top with remaining seasoning and wrap with the excess cloth. Reserve in the refrigerator for 18 hours.

Rinse the salmon under cold running water and transfer to a roasting rack. Set the rack in the refrigerator for an additional 18 hours. (This will cause a skin to form on the outside of the fish.)

Smoke the salmon with apple wood at 100 degrees for 5 hours.

FOR THE MARMALADE: Drizzle the oil in a large sauté pan and caramelize the onions, ginger, and garlic over medium heat. Deglaze the pan with red wine vinegar and wine. Continue to cook over medium heat. After the liquid has reduced by half, add the sugar and stir until dissolved. When the pan is dry, transfer the marmalade to a container and refrigerate until ready to serve.

FOR THE POTATO CRISP: Blanch the potatoes in salted boiling water for 10 seconds and then shock in an ice water bath. Drain the potatoes and dry thoroughly with a kitchen towel. Gently toss with cornstarch in a mixing bowl. Wrap the potatoes around several 4-inch metal ring molds.

Pour vegetable oil into a large, heavy pot or a deep-fryer and heat to 350 degrees. Fry the potatoes—still wrapped around the molds—in batches. After 4 minutes, or when the potatoes are golden brown, drain on a paper towel and season with salt. Cool to room temperature and remove the molds.

TO SERVE: Place a dollop of crème fraîche seasoned with chives in the center of each plate to secure the potato ring. Add several slices of smoked salmon and the red onion marmalade. Garnish with additional crème fraîche.

Makes 12 servings, with leftover salmon

*A rotating mandolin is similar to a standard Japanese mandolin, but is connected to a crank and produces curly-shaped strings of vegetables.

This is salmon on a bagel turned completely on its head. Rather than serving it with classic lox accoutrements, I use a dramatic halo of thin-cut potatoes and red onion marmalade. Make sure to cure the salmon at least three days in advance and have plenty of apple wood on hand for the smoking process.

Seared Foie Gras with Concord Grapes, Vanilla Pound Cake, and Poached Quince

VANILLA POUND CAKE

3 eggs

3 tablespoons milk

2 teaspoons vanilla extract

1 1/2 cups cake flour

3/4 cup sugar

1 teaspoon baking powder

1/8 teaspoon kosher salt

6 ounces unsalted butter, softened

QUINCE

1 quart Chardonnay

2 tablespoons sugar

1 tablespoon saffron

1 quince

CONCORD GRAPE SAUCE

375 milliliters Banyuls wine

2 tablespoons sugar

2 pounds Concord grapes

4 3-ounce pieces of foie gras

Kosher salt and black pepper, to taste

2 cups arugula

1 tablespoon lemon vinaigrette
(pg 164)

1 tablespoon parsley oil (pg 169),
in a squeeze bottle

FOR THE POUND CAKE: Preheat the oven to 350 degrees.

In a mixing bowl, combine the eggs, milk, and vanilla extract. Set aside.

In a stand-up mixer fitted with a paddle attachment, combine the flour, sugar, baking powder, and salt. Beat in the softened butter until the mixture is light and fluffy, about 2 minutes.

Pour in half the egg mixture and continue to beat on medium speed for 2 more minutes. Scrape down the sides of the bowl with a spatula and beat in the remaining egg mixture.

Fill a dozen 2-ounce tulip cups with the batter, and bake on a sheet pan for 15 minutes or until the tops are golden. If cooked properly, a toothpick should come out with only a few moist crumbs attached.

Foie gras is extremely rich, so I like to complement it with pound cake— for just the right amount of sweetness and contrast. I serve it with a Concord grape reduction and an aromatic fruit, like quince, which is best poached in aromatics a few days ahead—reserved in its own cooking liquid to enhance its flavor.

FOR THE QUINCE: In a sauce pot, reduce the wine, sugar, and saffron by three-fourths.

Peel the quince with a vegetable peeler. Using a Parisienne scoop, turn out quince rounds. Add the quince to the white wine reduction and simmer until tender, about 10 minutes or until easily pierced with a knife.

Pour the cooked quince and poaching liquid into a container and refrigerate for several hours. (This step will allow the saffron to penetrate, enhancing the flavor of the fruit.)

Recipe continued on page 46.

FOR THE CONCORD GRAPE SAUCE: In a saucepan, reduce the Banyuls and sugar by half. Add the Concord grapes and cook until the skins burst. Use an immersion blender to purée the grapes, then strain through a chinois.

TO COMPLETE: Warm the pound cakes slightly in the oven and discard the wrappers. Reheat the quince with its reserved poaching liquid in a small pot. In another small pot, warm the Concord grape reduction.

Season both sides of the foie gras with salt and pepper. Sear for 2 minutes in a heavy-bottomed pan over high heat. Flip over and continue to cook for 1 minute more or until golden brown on both sides.

Lightly dress the arugula with lemon vinaigrette and set aside.

TO SERVE: Place a piece of pound cake in the center of each serving bowl. Place 2 pieces of quince next to the cake and top with foie gras. Spoon 2 ounces of grape sauce around the plate. Garnish with a small bundle of arugula and drops of parsley oil.

Makes 4 servings
(Leftover pound cake can be frozen in an airtight container for up to 1 month.)

Beef Shabu-Shabu with Vermicelli Galette and Dried Mushroom Broth

DRIED MUSHROOM BROTH

1 quart water

1 6x6-inch piece of kombu seaweed

6 tablespoons soy sauce

1 tablespoon plus 1 teaspoon mirin

1/4 cup dried trumpet mushrooms

1 cup dried shiitake mushrooms

1 tablespoon bonito flakes

GALETTE

2 pounds vermicelli

Vegetable oil, for frying

6 ounces Kobe New York strip loin, cut into paper-thin slices

2 ounces diced foie gras

1 ounce sliced lion's mane mushrooms

1/4 cup dried corn

3 ounces daikon sprouts

6 cubes soy gelée (pg 165)

FOR THE DRIED MUSHROOM BROTH: Simmer the broth ingredients in a large pot for 5 minutes and let steep for 15 minutes more. Strain through a chinois—discarding the solids and reserving the broth.

FOR THE GALETTE: Boil the pasta according to package directions and discard the water. Do not rinse the pasta.

Spray a 9x5 baking sheet with nonstick spray, then spread the pasta out and stack about 3 inches high. Stack another baking sheet on top and weigh down with at least 3 pounds of cans. Allow the pasta to cool in the refrigerator overnight. Meanwhile, the natural starches will cause the noodles to stick together—creating a dense, compact sheet.

Use a 2-inch ring mold to cut the noodles. Set aside.

Shabu-shabu is a fantastic style of dining where meats and vegetables are cooked in a pot and their accumulated juices become the base—or the soup—of the dish. We top extravagantly marbled Kobe beef with an intensely flavored mushroom stock—enriched with the deep earthiness of trumpet and shiitake mushrooms.

TO COMPLETE: In a nonstick pan, sear the galettes in 1 tablespoon of vegetable oil, until both sides are golden brown. Meanwhile, bring the mushroom broth to a boil and reserve.

TO SERVE: Place a galette in the center of each serving bowl and surround with several slices of Kobe beef. Top with an assortment of diced foie gras, mushrooms, dried corn, daikon sprouts, and soy gelée. Ladle 4 ounces of hot broth over the top (which will cook the beef) and serve hot.

Makes 4 servings

Crispy Braised Pork Belly with Celery Root, Mandarin Orange Barbecue Sauce, Pickled Turnips, Daikon Sprouts, and Honey Sriracha

PORK BELLY

2 pounds pork belly

1 cup kosher salt

2 tablespoons sugar

2 tablespoons black pepper

6 minced thyme sprigs

2 quarts chicken stock (pg 166)

2 bay leaves

PICKLED TURNIPS

1 pound peeled and julienned turnips

1 cup water

3/4 cup rice vinegar

3/4 cup sugar

2 teaspoons kosher salt

1 whole clove

2 allspice berries

1 teaspoon mustard seed

1 teaspoon roasted black peppercorns

1 teaspoon chopped ginger

1 minced jalapeño, seeds removed

1 chopped shallot

CELERY ROOT

2 cups heavy cream

1/4 pound unsalted butter

2 cups water

1 peeled and diced celery root

Kosher salt, to taste

FOR THE PORK BELLY: Rub the pork belly with the salt, sugar, 1 tablespoon of pepper, and half of the thyme. Cover and refrigerate for 12 hours.

Rinse off the seasoning under cold running water. Pat dry. In a large, heavy pot, sear the pork over medium heat until golden brown on all sides. Pour out the excess fat and add the chicken stock, bay leaves, and the remaining pepper and thyme. Cover and simmer over low heat for 2 hours or until the pork is tender.

Remove the pork from the pot and place it on a sheet pan. Weigh down the pan with another sheet pan and at least 3 pounds of cans. Compress the pork belly in the refrigerator for 2 hours, then cut into 8 square pieces.

Creating a pork belly dish is a process that couldn't be more rewarding— especially when the pork is deep-fried and served crispy. Here, I toss it with lots of reduced citrus juice and soy sauce. It's my take on Japanese barbecue: sticky, sweet, and spiked with just a hint of sriracha.

FOR THE PICKLED TURNIPS: Place the turnips in a mixing bowl. In a sauce pot, bring the rest of the ingredients to a boil and then simmer for 5 minutes. Strain the liquid through a chinois over the bowl of turnips, and cover the bowl with plastic wrap. (The turnips will continue to cook as they soak in the liquid.) Refrigerate the mixture until ready to use.

FOR THE CELERY ROOT: Combine the cream, butter, and water in a sauce pot. Add the celery root and bring to a boil. Reduce to a simmer and cook until the celery root is tender, about 20 minutes. Strain the liquid, reserving the celery root and cooking liquid separately.

Purée the celery root in a food processor while still hot. Add just enough reserved cooking liquid to create a creamy consistency. Season with salt and pass through a tamis. Reserve warm.

Recipe and ingredients continued on page 52.

HONEY SRIRACHA

1/4 cup honey

1/4 cup sriracha chili sauce

MANDARIN ORANGE BARBECUE SAUCE

1 cup mandarin orange juice

1 cup soy sauce

3 garlic cloves, peeled

2 tablespoons sugar

1 tablespoon black vinegar

2 tablespoons sesame oil

1 tablespoon sesame seeds

1 teaspoon ground black pepper

1/2 teaspoon minced ginger

4 tablespoons cornstarch slurry (equal parts cornstarch and cold water combined)

PORK BELLY BATTER

Vegetable oil, for frying

1 1/2 cups all-purpose flour

1/2 cup cornstarch

1 tablespoon baking powder

2 cups seltzer water

1 egg

2 cups daikon sprouts, cut 1 inch from the top

8 mandarin orange segments

FOR THE HONEY SRIRACHA: Combine the honey and sriracha and set aside.

FOR THE MANDARIN ORANGE BARBECUE SAUCE: Combine all the ingredients, except the cornstarch slurry, in a sauce pot. Bring the mixture to a boil and reduce to a simmer. Add the cornstarch slurry and continue to simmer for another minute.

TO COMPLETE: Pour vegetable oil into a deep-fryer or a large, heavy pot and heat to 350 degrees.

Meanwhile, combine the pork belly batter ingredients in a bowl. (The flour should be well incorporated but not overworked.) Coat the pork belly in the batter, shaking off the excess. Plunge the pork into the hot oil and cook until golden brown and crispy, about 2 minutes for each batch.

While still warm, toss the pork with the mandarin orange barbecue sauce.

TO SERVE: Place a pool of the celery root purée in the center of each serving plate and top with a piece of pork belly. Garnish with 2 tablespoons of pickled turnips, 1/4 cup daikon sprouts, mandarin orange segments, and a drizzle of honey sriracha sauce.

Makes 8 servings

Minestrone with White Beans, Ricotta Tortellini, and Crispy Serrano Ham

BROTH
1/4 cup diced pancetta
1/4 cup extra virgin olive oil
1 cup diced onions
1/2 cup diced celery
1/4 cup diced carrot
3 garlic cloves, peeled
8 diced Roma tomatoes
1/4 cup tomato paste
1/2 cup Chardonnay
1 bay leaf
1 thyme sprig
1 oregano sprig
1/2 tablespoon red pepper flakes
1 gallon chicken stock (pg 166)

BEANS
1/2 cup navy beans
1 quart water
1 thyme sprig
2 garlic cloves, peeled and smashed
3 tablespoons extra virgin olive oil
Kosher salt and black pepper, to taste

RICOTTA CHEESE
1 quart whole milk
1/2 cup heavy cream
1/2 teaspoon kosher salt
3 tablespoons fresh-squeezed lemon juice

FOR THE BROTH: In a large sauté pan, render the pancetta in olive oil until crispy. Add the onions, celery, carrots, garlic, and tomatoes, and sweat until tender, about 5 minutes. Add the tomato paste and cook until fragrant. Deglaze the pan with wine and cook for another minute. Stir in the remaining ingredients and simmer for an additional 30 minutes. Strain the mixture through a chinois and discard the solids. Reserve the broth.

FOR THE BEANS: In the refrigerator, soak the beans in water overnight.

Fill a large pot with 1 quart of water and simmer the beans with thyme, garlic, and olive oil. After 1 hour, and just before the beans are fully cooked, season with salt and pepper. When the beans are completely tender, strain and pour them into a separate bowl. Set aside.

Gerardo Pasqualetti was a chef in the Netherland Plaza's kitchen for more than fifty-two years. He was, and is, a restaurant legend—a vibrant, thick-blooded Italian with a penchant for storytelling. To honor him at his retirement dinner, I recreated one of his favorite soups, staying true to its flavor profile but completely reimagining its presentation.

FOR THE RICOTTA CHEESE: Bring the milk, cream, and salt to a rolling boil in a medium quart sauce pot. Add the lemon juice and reduce the heat—mixing constantly until the liquid curdles, about 10 minutes more. Strain the mixture through a chinois lined with cheesecloth for 2 hours in the refrigerator.

FOR THE RICOTTA FILLING: Mix together all the ingredients in a bowl. Spoon the mixture into a pastry bag and set aside.

Recipe and ingredients continued on page 55.

RICOTTA FILLING

3 cups ricotta cheese

6 roasted garlic cloves
(pg 167), smashed

3 tablespoons chopped chives

1 tablespoon black pepper

2 egg yolks

Kosher salt, to taste

PASTA

2 cups all-purpose flour,
plus extra for dusting

1 egg, plus 8 egg yolks

2 teaspoons extra virgin olive oil

1 tablespoon kosher salt

1 tablespoon milk

SERRANO CHIPS

8 paper-thin slices of Serrano ham

PARMESAN CRISPS

1/4 cup grated Parmigiano-Reggiano

2 tablespoons chopped oregano

3 tablespoons tomato concassé
(pg 164)

3 tablespoons diced squash

3 tablespoons diced eggplant

1 tablespoon grated
Parmigiano-Reggiano

8 basil leaves, lightly fried
in vegetable oil

1 tablespoon extra virgin olive oil

FOR THE PASTA: Combine all the ingredients in a stand-up mixer fitted with a hook attachment. Beat on medium speed for 10 minutes. Knead for 15 minutes and refrigerate the dough for 1 hour.

Using a rolling pin, roll the dough into a paper-thin sheet. Cut out a series of 3-inch circles with a ring mold.

TO FORM THE RICOTTA TORTELLINI: Pipe 1 tablespoon of ricotta filling in the center of each circle. Use a pastry brush to paint half the dough with water. Fold the dough in half, creating a tight seal where the wet and dry dough meets—being careful to avoid air bubbles. Dip one corner of the dough in water, then fold it in half lengthwise, creating a tortellini shape. Place the tortellini on a flour-dusted sheet pan and reserve.

FOR THE SERRANO CHIPS: Preheat the oven to 225 degrees.

Spread the Serrano ham on a sheet pan lined with parchment paper. Bake until the ham starts to crisp, approximately 1 hour.

FOR THE PARMESAN CRISPS: Mix the cheese and oregano in a small bowl. Sprinkle in a nonstick pan and cook over medium heat until crispy, about 4 minutes.

TO COMPLETE: In a sauce pot, boil the tortellini for 3 minutes or until tender. Strain and reserve.

In a sauté pan, cook the tomato concassé, squash, and eggplant over high heat until tender, about 3 minutes. Add 1/4 cup of the cooked beans and the grated Parmigiano-Reggiano. Warm the tortellini in simmering water.

TO SERVE: Spoon 3 tablespoons of vegetables in the center of each of 8 serving bowls. Top with a tortellini, Serrano ham chip, fried basil leaf, and Parmesan crisp. Pour the broth over the top and finish with a drizzle of olive oil.

Makes 8 servings

Crab Bisque with Basmati Rice,
Salt and Pepper Crab, and Rice Cracker

SOUP

2 Dungeness crabs (reserving the leg meat for salt and pepper crab)

1 medium diced carrot

2 medium diced celery ribs

1 medium diced onion

3 minced garlic cloves

3 tablespoons tomato paste

2 bay leaves

2 tablespoons Madras curry

1 teaspoon cayenne pepper

1 cup brandy

1/4 cup Chardonnay wine

1 1/2 quarts water

2 thyme sprigs

2 cups cream

1/2 cup cooked basmati rice

Kosher salt and black pepper, to taste

BASMATI RICE

2 cups basmati rice

1 quart water

RICE CRACKER

1 cup reserved cooked basmati rice

Water, as needed

FOR THE SOUP: In a large stockpot, sweat the crab shells with the carrots, celery, onions, and garlic until translucent, about 10 minutes. Add the tomato paste, bay leaves, curry, and cayenne, and cook until fragrant, about 5 minutes more. Deglaze the pot with brandy and wine, and continue cooking until reduced by half. Add the water and thyme and reduce by half again, then add the cream and reduce by half once more. Strain the liquid through a chinois, and add the cooked basmati rice.

Purée the soup in a blender and strain, discarding the solids. Adjust the seasoning with salt and pepper. Reserve warm.

Crab bisque is typically a French preparation, but mine is rooted in the complex flavors of India. Edged in Madras curry and thickened with basmati rice, it has a delicate, warm aftertaste that's both comforting and intriguing.

FOR THE BASMATI RICE: Rinse the basmati rice under cold running water. Add the rice and water to a large pot and cook over high heat. When the rice starts to boil, cover it with a lid and reduce the heat. Simmer for 30-40 minutes, or until the rice is tender.

On a greased sheet pan, spread the rice out in a 1-inch-thick layer. Compact the rice by covering the pan with a layer of parchment paper and another heavy sheet pan. Refrigerate until the rice is set, about 1 hour. Set aside, reserving 1 cup of cold rice for the cracker in the following steps.

FOR THE RICE CRACKER: Preheat a convection oven to 200 degrees.

Add the reserved cooked rice to a small saucepan. Cook the rice over low heat, adding water as necessary until the rice is overcooked and falling apart. Smash the rice using the back of a spoon.

Spread the rice over a silpat with a bowl scraper or a rubber spatula—creating a paper-thin layer. With the convection oven fan turned on, bake the rice for 1 hour or until crispy and completely dehydrated.

Remove from the oven and let cool. Using a 1-inch ring mold, cut the rice into a series of circles and set aside.

Recipe and ingredients continued on page 58.

SALT AND PEPPER CRAB

2 tablespoons finely ground black pepper

1 tablespoon kosher salt

1 1/2 cups all-purpose flour

1/2 cup cornstarch

1 tablespoon baking powder

2 cups seltzer water

1 egg

Reserved Dungeness crab legs, separated into 16 pieces

Vegetable oil, for frying

Kosher salt, to taste

1 tablespoon micro chives

2 tablespoons curry oil (pg 165)

FOR THE SALT AND PEPPER CRAB: Make the batter by combining the first 7 ingredients, being careful not to overwork the flour. Coat the crab in the batter, shaking off the excess.

Pour vegetable oil into a deep-fryer or a large, heavy pot and heat to 350 degrees. Fry the crab in batches for 3 to 5 minutes or until puffy and golden brown. Drain on a paper towel, season with salt, and reserve hot.

TO SERVE: Cut the basmati rice into 2-inch rounds and warm. Place rounds in the center of each serving bowl. Top with 2 pieces of fried crab and a rice cracker, and garnish with micro chives. Pour in the crab bisque, and drizzle with curry oil.

Makes 8 servings

Oyster Velouté with Sweetbreads, Tapioca Pearls, and Kusshi Oysters

VELOUTÉ

10 rinsed Kusshi oysters

2 chopped celery ribs

1/2 chopped fennel bulb

1 chopped leek, white parts only

5 chopped shallots

1/4 cup plus 2 tablespoons unsalted butter

1 bottle Sauvignon Blanc

1/2 bottle Champagne

10 ounces clam juice

4 bay leaves

3 peppercorns

1 cup heavy cream, plus 2 tablespoons whipped to soft peaks

SWEETBREADS

1 sweetbread lobe

2 cups milk

2 egg whites, whipped

1/4 cup chopped leeks

1/4 cup chopped celery

2 ounces shiitake mushroom stems

2 chopped shallots

3 tablespoons unsalted butter

1 thyme sprig

1 bay leaf

1 tablespoon peppercorns

1 cup Chardonnay

2 quarts vegetable stock

FOR THE VELOUTÉ: Using an oyster knife, carefully pop the oyster shells open and remove the meat. Reserve the meat and shells separately.

In a large pot, sweat the celery, fennel, leeks, and shallots in 1/4 cup of butter until tender, about 10 minutes. Add the oyster shells, wine, and Champagne. Bring the liquid to a boil, reduce to a simmer, and cook until the liquid is reduced by half, about 15 minutes. Add the clam juice, bay leaves, and peppercorns, and simmer until the liquid is reduced by half again. Add 1 cup heavy cream, bring the liquid to a boil, and remove from heat.

Through a chinois, strain the mixture into a blender. Add the oyster meat, reserving 4 for later use, and purée on high. Strain the soup again and refrigerate in an airtight container until ready to serve.

For me, this velouté is as close to perfection as I have ever come. It's made by reducing oyster shells and Champagne together—two components with a natural affinity for one another. Sweetbreads anchor the rich flavors of the dish—and for the garnish I use playful pearls of tapioca.

FOR THE SWEETBREADS: Remove the excess sinew from the sweetbreads and discard. Soak the sweetbreads in milk overnight.

Transfer the sweetbreads to a mixing bowl with the egg whites and soak for 15 minutes. Use plastic wrap to roll the sweetbreads into a tight cylinder—tying the ends of the roll into knots. Set aside.

In a large pot, sweat the leeks, celery, mushrooms, and shallots in unsalted butter until tender, about 5 minutes. Add the thyme, bay leaf, peppercorns, and wine. Continue to cook until the liquid is reduced by three-fourths, about 15 minutes. Add the vegetable stock and simmer for 10 minutes more.

Recipe and ingredients continued on page 62.

Kosher salt and white pepper, to taste
All-purpose flour, for dredging
2 tablespoons clarified butter
1/4 cup red wine vinegar
Sea salt, to taste

TAPIOCA

1 gallon plus 2 tablespoons water
1/2 cup kosher salt
1 cup tapioca pearls

4 purple potato chips (pg 168)
1 tablespoon sliced chives

To ensure that the sweetbreads absorb the poaching liquid, poke holes in the plastic wrap with a knife. Add the sweetbreads to the simmering vegetable stock and cook for 12 minutes.

Remove the sweetbreads and use a new sheet of plastic to rewrap them into a tight cylinder. Let them cool in the refrigerator for at least 4 hours.

FOR THE TAPIOCA: In a large pot, simmer 1 gallon of water and the salt. Add the tapioca pearls and cook gently for 20 minutes or until the tapioca is tender. Strain through a chinois and reserve.

TO COMPLETE: Slice the sweetbreads into 2-inch pieces, and season with salt and white pepper. Dredge in flour, shaking off the excess.

Sear the sweetbreads over medium heat in a sauté pan with clarified butter. After 3 minutes, flip the sweetbreads and continue to cook until golden brown on both sides, about 3 minutes more. Remove the pan from the heat, pour out the excess fat, and deglaze with 1/4 cup of red wine vinegar. Simmer until the vinegar has evaporated. Season again with sea salt.

Reheat the soup and purée it with 2 tablespoons of unsalted butter and 2 tablespoons of whipped heavy cream. Reserve hot.

Warm the tapioca gently with 2 tablespoons of water.

Warm the 4 reserved oysters on a baking sheet under the broiler for 20 seconds.

TO SERVE: Place the sweetbreads in the center of each soup bowl and top with a kusshi oyster. Pour the soup into the bowl, and garnish with a purple potato chip and a pinch of chives. Finish with tapioca and serve immediately.

Makes 4 servings

Blue Cheese Beignets with Local Honey, Frisée, Belgian Endive, and Almond Brittle

BLUE CHEESE BEIGNETS

5 ounces milk

2 1/4 ounces unsalted butter

4 ounces all-purpose flour

4 eggs

1 tablespoon chopped thyme

4 ounces blue cheese

Kosher salt, to taste

Vegetable oil, for frying

RED WINE VINAIGRETTE

1 chopped shallot

1 tablespoon Dijon mustard

1/2 cup red wine vinegar

1 1/2 cups vegetable oil

Kosher salt and black pepper, to taste

ALMOND BRITTLE

1/2 cup sugar

1/4 cup light corn syrup

1 tablespoon brown sugar

1 tablespoon unsalted butter, softened

1 teaspoon kosher salt

1/4 cup sliced almonds

FOR THE BLUE CHEESE BEIGNETS: In a small sauce pot, warm the milk and butter over medium heat. Whisk in the flour, and cook over low heat until the mixture begins to stick to the sides of the pot.

Transfer to a stand-up mixer fitted with a paddle attachment and beat the dough for 1 minute. Add the eggs, one at a time, then add the thyme and blue cheese. Season with salt and set aside.

FOR THE RED WINE VINAIGRETTE: Purée the shallots, Dijon mustard, and vinegar in a blender. With the motor running, slowly drizzle in the oil. Season to taste with salt and pepper.

Traditionally, a beignet is deep-fried dough covered with powdered sugar and served as a dessert. In this savory application, I fill it with rich blue cheese and serve it with bitter greens, almond brittle, and spiced honey harvested from our rooftop beehive.

FOR THE ALMOND BRITTLE: Preheat the oven to 350 degrees and line a baking sheet with parchment paper.

In a bowl, mix together the sugar, corn syrup, brown sugar, butter, and salt. Fold in the nuts. Divide the mixture into a series of quarter-sized pieces and transfer to the baking sheet. Bake for 15 minutes.

FOR THE SPICED HONEY: Toast the spices in a sauté pan, add the honey, and cook until the mixture is fragrant, about 2 minutes. Cool to room temperature and add the Banyuls vinegar. Strain and set aside.

Recipe and ingredients continued on page 66.

SPICED HONEY

1/2 ounce black pepper

3 cardamom pods

6 spice berries

2 cloves

3/4 ounce cumin

1/4 ounce fennel seeds

4 ounces local honey

1 1/2 ounces Banyuls vinegar

1 head Belgian endive

1 head radicchio

1 head frisée

2 ounces crumbled blue cheese

Kosher salt and black pepper, to taste

TO COMPLETE: Pour vegetable oil into a large, heavy pot or a deep-fryer and heat to 325 degrees. Use an ice cream scoop to plunge the beignet batter into the oil. Fry until golden brown, about 3 minutes.

Toss the lettuces with blue cheese and red wine vinaigrette. Season with salt and pepper.

TO SERVE: Drizzle the spiced honey on the bottom of each salad plate. Place the beignets on top. Garnish with mixed lettuce and a piece of the almond brittle.

Makes 6 servings

Grilled Ramp Tortellini with Morel Mushrooms, Arugula, and Roasted Garlic Butter Sauce

PASTA

2 cups all-purpose flour,
plus extra for dusting

1 egg, plus 8 egg yolks

2 teaspoons extra virgin olive oil

1 tablespoon kosher salt

1 tablespoon milk

RICOTTA CHEESE

1 quart whole milk

1/2 cup heavy cream

1/2 teaspoon kosher salt

3 tablespoons lemon juice

RAMP FILLING

28 ramps

2 tablespoons extra virgin olive oil

Kosher salt and black pepper, to taste

3 roasted garlic cloves
(pg 167), smashed

2 cups ricotta cheese

ROASTED GARLIC BUTTER SAUCE

1/4 cup water

6 roasted garlic cloves
(pg 167), smashed

1/2 pound unsalted butter, cold

Kosher salt, to taste

FOR THE PASTA: Combine all the ingredients in a stand-up mixer fitted with a hook attachment. Beat on medium speed for 10 minutes. Knead the dough for 15 minutes and refrigerate for 1 hour.

FOR THE RICOTTA CHEESE: In a sauce pot, bring the milk, cream, and salt to a rolling boil. Add the lemon juice and reduce the heat to low—mixing constantly until the liquid curdles, about 10 minutes more. Strain the mixture through a chinois lined with cheesecloth for at least 2 hours in the refrigerator.

Ramps have an unbelievable, wild onion flavor. They only grow for a few weeks of the year in climates with cold nights and hot days, making them a prized commodity in the early spring. This is a simple dish that highlights their delicate flavors in fresh tortellini—folded with ricotta cheese and topped with morel mushrooms.

FOR THE RAMP FILLING: Boil the ramps in a sauce pot with salted water for 1 minute or just until tender. Shock in an ice bath to stop the cooking process.

In a mixing bowl, toss 20 ramps with olive oil, salt, and pepper, reserving 8 ramps to complete the dish. Grill for 1 minute or until slightly charred. Mince as fine as possible, then combine with the garlic and ricotta cheese. Season with salt and pepper.

TO FORM THE TORTELLINI: Using a rolling pin, roll the dough into a paper-thin sheet. Cut out a series of 3-inch circles with a ring mold.

Place 1/2 tablespoon of ramp filling in the center of each circle. Use a pastry brush to paint half the dough with water. Fold in half, creating a tight seal where the wet and dry dough meets—being careful to avoid air bubbles. Dip one corner of the dough in water, then fold it in half lengthwise, creating a tortellini. Transfer to a flour-dusted sheet pan and reserve.

Recipe and ingredients continued on page 69.

MUSHROOMS

2 tablespoons unsalted butter

1 cup morel mushrooms

1 diced shallot

Kosher salt and black pepper, to taste

8 ramps (previously reserved)

1/2 cup arugula

2 tablespoons minced chives

3 ounces shaved Parmigiano-Reggiano

2 tablespoons black truffle oil

FOR THE ROASTED GARLIC BUTTER SAUCE: In a saucepan, bring the water and roasted garlic to a boil. After 1 minute, reduce the heat and continue to simmer.

Gently whip in the cold butter—whisking constantly until emulsified. (Do not let the butter mixture get too warm or the emulsification will break.) Strain the liquid through a chinois and season with salt. Reserve warm in the pot.

FOR THE MUSHROOMS: Melt the butter in a sauté pan and add the mushrooms. Once lightly cooked, add the shallots and cook 1 minute more. Season with salt and pepper.

TO COMPLETE: Grill the 8 reserved ramps until charred.

In a sauce pot, boil the tortellini for 3 minutes or until tender. Toss them with the roasted garlic sauce, mushroom mixture, arugula, and chives.

TO SERVE: Place 4 tortellini in each serving bowl and top with grilled ramps. Garnish with shaved Parmigiano-Reggiano and a drizzle of truffle oil.

Makes 8 servings

Mâche Salad with Port Wine Yuzu Vinaigrette, Brie and Fig Grilled Cheese, and Candied Huckleberries

HUCKLEBERRIES

1/2 cup huckleberries

1 cup sugar

GRILLED CHEESE

1 cup dried figs, stems removed

1 quart ruby port wine

1 baguette

1 pound brie, rind removed

3 tablespoons unsalted butter

Kosher salt, to taste

PORT WINE YUZU DRESSING

1 cup port wine

1/4 cup yuzu juice

2 egg yolks

3/4 cup honey

3 tablespoons Dijon mustard

1 1/2 cups vegetable oil

PORT WINE HIBISCUS REDUCTION

1 bottle ruby port wine

1 cup dried hibiscus flowers

2 heads mâche

FOR THE HUCKLEBERRIES: In a small bowl, toss the huckleberries with the sugar. Lay the huckleberries out on a sheet tray and freeze.

FOR THE GRILLED CHEESE: Cut the figs in half lengthwise. Soak in a small pot with port wine for 1 hour. Simmer the liquid until reduced by three-fourths. Strain through a chinois and reserve the cooking liquid separately.

Purée the figs in a food processor, and add the reserved cooking liquid, as needed, to form a smooth paste. Set the mixture aside.

Slice the baguette on a bias into several half-inch pieces. To create each sandwich, spread one piece of bread with fig jam and brie cheese. Top with another slice of bread and set aside.

The rich flavor of this sandwich relies on high-quality ingredients. Start by slathering a purée of figs on a slice of fresh baguette—and top it with gooey brie cheese and another slice of bread. Finish with mâche lettuce, dressed lightly in a reduction of port wine and tangy yuzu juice.

FOR THE PORT WINE YUZU DRESSING: Reduce the port wine by half in a small sauce pot. Transfer to a blender and add the yuzu, egg yolks, honey, and Dijon mustard. With the motor running, slowly drizzle in the vegetable oil until the dressing is emulsified.

FOR THE PORT WINE HIBISCUS REDUCTION: In a saucepan, reduce the port wine and hibiscus flowers until thick and syrupy. Strain the liquid through a chinois and refrigerate until needed.

TO COMPLETE: Melt the butter in a large sauté pan, and cook the sandwich for 2 minutes over low heat. Flip and brown the other side, 2 minutes more. Season with salt and cut through the center on a bias.

In a separate bowl, lightly toss the mâche lettuce in port wine yuzu vinaigrette.

TO SERVE: Using a pastry brush, paint the plate with a streak of port wine hibiscus reduction. Place the grilled cheese on top and garnish with the mâche lettuce. Sprinkle with frozen huckleberries.

Makes 4 servings

English Pea Purée with Fava Beans, White and Green Asparagus, Tarragon, and Parmesan Cheese

ENGLISH PEA PURÉE

2 cups shelled English peas

1/4 cup extra virgin olive oil

1/4 cup chicken stock
(pg 166), warmed

3 tablespoons chopped tarragon

Kosher salt and black pepper, to taste

SPRING VEGETABLES

8 green asparagus spears

8 white asparagus spears

8 ramps

1/4 cup shelled English peas

1/4 cup fava beans

2 tablespoons extra virgin olive oil

Kosher salt and black pepper, to taste

1 diced shallot

3 ounces Parmigiano-Reggiano, shaved

8 sliced French breakfast radishes

1/4 cup micro flowers

1 tablespoon black truffle oil

FOR THE PEA PURÉE: In a sauce pot, blanch the peas in salted, boiling water until tender, about 2 minutes. Strain and discard the liquid. While still hot, purée the peas in a blender with the remaining ingredients. Pass the purée through a tamis and reserve.

This dish is a celebration of spring—one of the most exciting seasons for me in the kitchen. Ramps and asparagus are usually the first ingredients to arrive, and I love to highlight their natural fresh flavors. Here, they're blanched and stacked over a vibrant purée of English peas.

FOR THE VEGETABLES: Snap the ends off the asparagus, reserving the tips. Peel with a vegetable peeler and blanch in salted, boiling water for 3 minutes or until tender. Plunge in an ice bath until cool, strain and reserve.

Blanch the ramps in boiling water for 1 minute, then shock in an ice water bath. Repeat the same process for the reserved English peas and fava beans, separately.

Toss the ramps in 1 tablespoon of olive oil and sprinkle with salt and pepper. Place them on a hot grill for 1 minute or until slightly charred.

In a pan over medium heat, sauté the shallots in 1 tablespoon of olive oil until translucent. Combine with the rest of the vegetables and season with salt and pepper.

TO COMPLETE: Reheat the pea purée in a small pot. Use a serving spoon to ribbon the purée on each plate. Place the remaining vegetables on top. Garnish with a long, thin slice of Parmigiano-Reggiano, radishes, micro flowers, and a drizzle of truffle oil.

Makes 4 servings

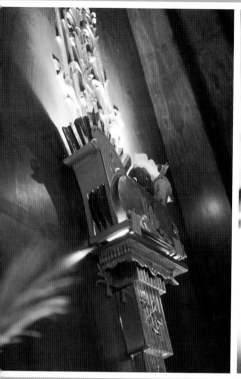

ENTRÉES

Inspiration for the main course can come from anywhere. Farmers markets. Books. Coffee shops. My eyes are always watching. My ears are always listening. Sometimes it's about reinterpreting an old classic. Other times it's about inventing an entirely new flavor profile with unexpected combinations. But it's always about a commitment to quality. Pasta rolled by hand. Mushrooms still freckled with dirt. Heirloom pigs raised by local farmers. It's a simple philosophy—but when it's time to eat, it's what draws the great divide between delicious and extraordinary.

Seared Truffle-Marinated Tuna with Wilted Brussels Sprouts, Smoked Bacon, Soy Gelée, and Worcestershire Aioli

WORCESTERSHIRE AIOLI

2 egg yolks

2 tablespoons Worcestershire sauce

2 tablespoons red wine vinegar

1 teaspoon lemon juice

2 1/2 cups vegetable oil

Kosher salt and black pepper, to taste

TUNA

1 cup white miso

1/2 cup soy sauce

1 tablespoon lime zest

2 tablespoons truffle juice

1/2 cup truffle oil

10 limes, juiced

10 roasted garlic cloves (pg 167)

6 fillets #1 sushi-grade tuna, about 5 ounces each

2 tablespoons vegetable oil

BRUSSELS SPROUTS

3 pounds Brussels sprouts

4 ounces diced smoked bacon

2 minced shallots

1/4 cup red wine vinegar

CRISPED SWEET POTATOES

1 sweet potato

Vegetable oil, for frying

2 tablespoons soy gelée (pg 165)

FOR THE WORCESTERSHIRE AIOLI: In a blender, combine the first 4 ingredients, and mix until well incorporated. With the motor running, slowly stream in the oil until emulsified. Season with salt and pepper.

FOR THE TUNA MARINADE: Combine the first 7 ingredients in a blender and mix well. Refrigerate the tuna in the marinade for 3 hours.

FOR THE BRUSSELS SPROUTS: Cut the ends off the Brussels sprouts and separate the leaves.

Render the bacon in a large sauté pan until crispy. Add the shallots and Brussels sprout leaves and gently wilt, about 1 minute. Deglaze the pan with red wine vinegar, remove from heat, and reserve warm.

FOR THE SWEET POTATOES: Peel the sweet potato and cut it into thin slices using a rotating mandolin.* Pour vegetable oil into a large, heavy pot or a deep-fryer and heat to 300 degrees. Fry the potato slices in batches until crispy but not yet brown, about 1 minute for each batch.

TO COMPLETE: Remove the tuna from the marinade. In a hot sauté pan with 2 tablespoons of vegetable oil, sear the tuna on one side for 30 seconds. Flip the tuna and sear for 30 seconds more, or until the outside is caramelized. Remove from heat and reserve.

TO SERVE: Place 2 ounces of wilted Brussels sprouts in the center of each plate and top with a piece of seared tuna. Garnish with Worcestershire aioli, soy gelée, and fried sweet potatoes.

Makes 6 servings

A rotating mandolin is similar to a standard Japanese mandolin, but is connected to a crank and produces curly-shaped strings of vegetables.

A marinade is an excellent way to infuse flavor into fish. But even after several hours, it doesn't penetrate all the way to the center of the cut. That's why I serve my seared tuna with a streak of Worcestershire aioli and several small cubes of soy gelée. This way, diners can season their fish as they go—adding richness and salt into every bite.

Gulf Snapper "en Papillote" with Vidalia Onions, Curry Vinaigrette, and Green Apple Tzatziki

SNAPPER

4 tablespoons unsalted butter

4 sliced green garlic

1 medium chopped Vidalia onion

2 chopped thyme sprigs

2 chopped leeks

Kosher salt and black pepper, to taste

8 sheets bric dough

1 pound red snapper, skin removed

8 tablespoons clarified butter

CURRY VINAIGRETTE

7 ounces cider vinegar

3 ounces orange juice

2 ounces lemon juice

1 1/2 ounces honey

1 ounce chopped garlic

1 ounce chopped lemongrass

2 cups curry oil (pg 165)

TZATZIKI SAUCE

2 cups plain yogurt, drained in a colander for 1 hour

6 chopped garlic cloves

1 julienned English cucumber

1/2 lemon, juiced

1 tablespoon extra virgin olive oil

Kosher salt and black pepper, to taste

FOR THE SNAPPER: In 1 tablespoon of butter, sweat the garlic over low heat until tender and translucent, about 5 minutes. Cool to room temperature and reserve.

Heat 1 tablespoon of butter and sauté the Vidalia onions over medium to medium-high heat. Cook for 5 minutes or until just tender. Add the chopped thyme and stir to incorporate. Remove the pan from heat and cool to room temperature.

In a small sauce pot with a lid, melt the remaining 2 tablespoons of butter and add the leeks. Cook over very low heat for 20 minutes or until all the moisture is released and the leeks are very tender. Transfer the leeks and their accumulated liquid to a blender and purée until smooth. Season with salt and pepper.

Lay the bric dough out flat and cut out a series of circles—the same size as your serving plates.

Cut the snapper on a bias into 2-ounce portions. Place a portion of snapper on the lower half of each piece of bric dough. Season the fish with salt and pepper. Spread a thin layer of leek purée over the top of the fish, followed by a spoonful each of green garlic and onions. Fold the top of the bric dough over the fish to create a half-moon shape.

Instead of using parchment paper for fish "en papillote," I wrap snapper in bric dough and let it steam as the dough crips. It's a technique I learned as a young chef working at Rubicon in San Francisco. The fish comes out perfect every time—moist on the inside, and golden brown and crispy on the outside.

FOR THE CURRY VINAIGRETTE: In a blender, purée the vinegar, orange juice, lemon juice, honey, garlic, and lemongrass. With the motor running, slowly drizzle in the curry oil, and continue to purée until smooth.

Recipe and ingredients continued on page 80.

  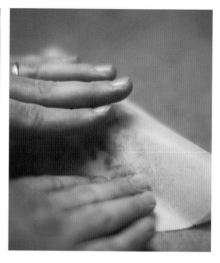

APPLE SALAD

2 julienned Granny Smith apples

1/4 cup micro red cabbage

2 tablespoons lemon
vinaigrette (pg 164)

Kosher salt and black pepper, to taste

FOR THE TZATZIKI SAUCE: In a mixing bowl, toss the yogurt, garlic, cucumber, and lemon juice with 1 tablespoon of olive oil. Season to taste with salt and pepper.

FOR THE APPLE SALAD: In a separate mixing bowl, toss the apples and micro cabbage with 2 tablespoons of lemon vinaigrette. Season to taste with salt and pepper.

TO COMPLETE: Cook 2 portions of fish over medium-high heat with 2 tablespoons of clarified butter. Flip the fish when the underside turns golden brown, and continue to cook 3 minutes more. Repeat this process until all of the fish is cooked through.

TO SERVE: Drizzle a thin layer of curry vinaigrette over the center of each plate. Top with 2 pieces of snapper en papillote. Line the center of the fish with cucumber tzatziki. Top with the apple salad.

Makes 4 servings

Seared Scallops with Sweet Corn, Baby Carrots, Crispy Mirin-Glazed Pork Belly, Quail Eggs, Almonds, and Curry Oil

PORK BELLY

1/4 cup sugar

1/4 cup kosher salt

1/8 teaspoon tinted cure mix

1 pound pork belly

1 1/2 cups all-purpose flour

1/2 cup cornstarch

1 tablespoon baking powder

2 cups seltzer water

1 egg

Vegetable oil, for frying

Kosher salt and black pepper, to taste

POLENTA

4 ears of corn

2 tablespoons polenta

3 tablespoons unsalted butter

Kosher salt and black pepper, to taste

MIRIN GLAZE

1/2 cup soy sauce

1/2 cup mirin

1/4 cup sugar

1/4 cup sake

1 inch chopped ginger

1/4 cup water plus 2 tablespoons cornstarch for slurry

FOR THE PORK BELLY: Mix together the sugar, salt, and tinted cure mix. Coat the pork belly in this mixture and cure in the refrigerator for 2 days.

Preheat the oven to 225 degrees. Remove the pork from the refrigerator and rinse off the seasoning under cold running water.

Roast the pork belly for 4 hours on a roasting rack until tender and golden brown. If the outside of the pork starts to turn dark brown too early, cover with foil for the remainder of its cooking time. Remove the pork from the oven, and cool the pork to room temperature. Slice into 1-ounce pieces and set aside.

Create a batter by combining the flour, cornstarch, baking powder, seltzer water, and egg in a mixing bowl. Stir until the flour is well incorporated but not overworked.

Pour vegetable oil into a large, heavy pot or a deep-fryer and heat to 375 degrees. Dredge the pork bellies in the tempura batter, shaking off any excess. Fry in batches for 2 minutes or until golden brown. Drain on a paper towel. Season with salt and pepper.

There are a lot of components in this dish, but all of them work together to create a careful balance of flavor and texture. I use puréed sweet corn with a little polenta to form a creamy base for the scallops. Then I add pork belly— glazed in an Asian-inspired mirin sauce for the perfect combination of sweetness and salt.

FOR THE POLENTA: Using a sharp knife, cut the kernels off the corncobs and reserve in a small bowl. Run the back of your knife across the length of the scraped corncobs, making sure to catch the "milk" in the bowl. Transfer to a blender and purée.

Recipe and ingredients continued on page 83.

CARROTS

12 baby carrots

1 thyme sprig

2 tablespoons unsalted butter

Kosher salt and black pepper, to taste

ALMONDS

1 tablespoons unsalted butter

1/4 cup sliced almonds

Kosher salt and black pepper, to taste

12 dry-packed sea scallops

Kosher salt and black pepper, to taste

2 tablespoons clarified butter

4 quail eggs

1/2 tablespoon unsalted butter

2 tablespoons curry oil (pg 165), in a squeeze bottle

1/4 cup micro greens

3 tablespoons dried corn

In a small pot, bring the mixture to a light simmer and slowly whisk in the polenta. Continue to cook the polenta over low heat until thickened. Swirl in the butter, and season with salt and pepper. If the corn seems too thick and starchy, add a few tablespoons of water.

FOR THE MIRIN GLAZE: Combine the soy sauce, mirin, sugar, sake, and ginger in a small saucepan. Bring to a light boil and reduce to a simmer. Continue to cook for 5 more minutes. Whisk in the cornstarch slurry and continue to cook 3 minutes more. Remove the pot from the heat, strain the liquid through a chinois, and let the glaze cool to room temperature.

FOR THE CARROTS: Simmer the carrots, thyme, butter, salt, and pepper in a pot of simmering water for 12 minutes.

FOR THE ALMONDS: Melt 1 tablespoon of butter in a pan over low heat. Add the almonds and cook until lightly toasted, about 3 minutes. Season with salt and pepper. Reserve warm.

TO COMPLETE: Blot the scallops dry with a paper towel, and season with salt and pepper. Sear on one side in a very hot sauté pan with 2 tablespoons of clarified butter. After about 3 minutes, flip the scallops and continue to cook for another 2 minutes. Remove the scallops from the pan and reserve warm.

In a separate pan, fry the quail eggs in 1/2 tablespoon of butter over medium heat. Cook the eggs sunny-side-up until whites are set.

TO SERVE: Place a ribbon of polenta in the center of each serving plate. Arrange 3 scallops on top. Drizzle the pork belly with mirin glaze and place 1 between each scallop (2 pieces of pork total). Top one scallop with a quail egg.

Arrange 3 carrots diagonally across the scallops and pork belly. Drizzle the plate with curry oil, and garnish with micro greens, almonds, and dried corn.

Makes 4 servings

Poached Halibut with Sunchokes, Haricots Verts, Dungeness Crab, and Tarragon

BEURRE BLANC

3 chopped shallots

3 cups Chardonnay

1 bay leaf

2 thyme sprigs

1 tablespoon black pepper

1 tablespoon rice wine vinegar

1 pound unsalted butter

1 lemon, juiced

Kosher salt and black pepper, to taste

SUNCHOKES

1 pound peeled sunchokes

1 quart water

1 quart heavy cream

Kosher salt, to taste

HALIBUT

4 pieces of halibut, 5 ounces each

Kosher salt and white pepper, to taste

1 quart fish fumet

HARICOTS VERTS

8 ounces haricots verts

1 tablespoon unsalted butter

1 chopped shallot

Kosher salt and black pepper, to taste

CRISPED SWEET POTATOES

1 sweet potato

Vegetable oil, for frying

8 ounces Dungeness crab leg meat

2 tablespoons chopped tarragon

FOR THE BEURRE BLANC: In a medium pot, combine the shallots, wine, bay leaf, thyme, pepper, and vinegar. Reduce to 3 tablespoons over medium-high heat. Lower the heat and slowly whisk in the butter and lemon juice. Season the sauce to taste with salt, pepper, and more lemon juice. Strain through a chinois and reserve in a warm part of the kitchen.

FOR THE SUNCHOKES: Place the sunchokes in a large pot with the water and cream. Season with salt, and boil until the sunchokes are tender, about 20 minutes.

Strain the sunchokes, reserving the cooking liquid separately. Press the sunchokes through a tamis. Incorporate the reserved cooking liquid as needed until the sunchokes are creamy. Check for seasoning and reserve warm.

FOR THE HALIBUT: Season the halibut with salt and white pepper. Transfer to a large sauté pan and cover with cold fish fumet.

Gently poach the halibut over low heat until just cooked through, about 10 minutes, depending on the thickness of the fish. Reserve warm.

FOR THE HARICOTS VERTS: In a pot of salted water, boil the haricots verts for 1 minute. Remove the beans from the pot and strain through a chinois. Transfer the beans to a hot sauté pan and add the butter and shallots. Cook over medium heat until tender, and season with salt and pepper.

FOR THE SWEET POTATOES: Peel the sweet potato and cut it into thin slices using a rotating mandolin.* Pour the vegetable oil into a large, heavy pot or a deep-fryer and heat to 300 degrees. Fry the potato slices in batches until crispy but not yet brown, about 1 minute for each batch.

TO COMPLETE: Fold in the crab and tarragon to the beurre blanc.

TO SERVE: Place a quenelle of sunchokes on each plate and top with haricots verts. Place the halibut over the beans and top with beurre blanc. Garnish with 2 pieces of crab and sweet potato crisps.

Makes 4 servings

*A rotating mandolin is similar to a standard Japanese mandolin, but is connected to a crank and produces curly-shaped strings of vegetables.

Poaching is a very simple, very delicate way to cook halibut, and it lends to a soft, buttery texture. The key to this dish is the beurre blanc—an emulsified butter sauce, enhanced with the bright, licorice flavor of tarragon. I use sunchokes here, for a comforting texture that's similar to mashed potatoes but with an unexpected floral quality.

Potato-Wrapped Salmon with Ham Hock Broth, Cipollini Onions, Dried Cherries, and Lovage

HAM HOCK BROTH

2 pork shanks

All-purpose flour, for dusting

2 tablespoons clarified butter

2 pig feet

2 smoked ham hocks

1 chopped parsnip

1 chopped celery rib

3 chopped shallots

6 chopped garlic cloves

2 bay leaves

2 bottles Sauvignon Blanc

5 chopped mushrooms

2 quarts chicken stock (pg 166)

Red wine vinegar, to taste

SALMON

1 gallon water

1 cup brown sugar

1 cup kosher salt

6 fillets of wild salmon, about 5 ounces each, skins removed

2 baking potatoes

3 tablespoons vegetable oil

FOR THE HAM HOCK BROTH: Dust the pork shanks in flour, shaking off any excess. Transfer to a hot sauté pan coated in 2 tablespoons of clarified butter. Caramelize the pork on all sides, 5 minutes total. Add the remaining ingredients, minus the stock and vinegar, and reduce by half.

Add the chicken stock and simmer over low heat for 2 hours or until the shanks are cooked through and falling off the bone. Remove the shanks and save for another use. Strain the stock and return the liquid to the pot. Reduce by one third over medium heat. Season to taste with red wine vinegar. Meanwhile, pull the meat from the smoked ham hocks and reserve.

Salmon, wrapped in thin slices of potato and caramelized in a hot sauté pan, is a visually stunning presentation. For complexity and depth of flavor, I serve it with a smoky ham hock broth, thickened to a light sauce consistency. Then I rest it simply on a bed of Brussels sprouts with cipollini onions and dried cherries.

FOR THE SALMON: Bring 1 gallon of water to a boil in a large pot. Add the sugar and salt, and stir until dissolved. Refrigerate the brine for 2 hours or until completely cool.

Add the salmon to the brine and continue to refrigerate for 4 hours. Remove the salmon from the brine and smoke for 1 hour in a cold smoker with apple wood. (Make sure the temperature of the box never exceeds 100 degrees.)

Peel the potatoes and spin on a rotating mandolin.* Blanch in salted boiling water and shock in an ice bath.

Carefully wrap each salmon fillet with the potato strings. Shallow-fry in a small sauté pan with 3 tablespoons of vegetable oil. Sauté over medium heat for 2 minutes on each side, or until the potatoes are crispy and the salmon is cooked medium.

Recipe and ingredients continued on page 88.

BRUSSELS SPROUT SALAD

4 cipollini onions
2 tablespoons extra virgin olive oil
Kosher salt and black pepper, to taste
5 Brussels sprouts
1/4 cup dried cherries
3 tablespoons thinly sliced lovage

FOR THE BRUSSELS SPROUT SALAD: Preheat the oven to 350 degrees.

Peel the onions and toss with olive oil, salt, and pepper. Roast until tender.

Trim the ends off the Brussels sprouts and separate the leaves. Combine in a sauce pot with the dried cherries, lovage, cipollini onions, and reserved ham hock meat. Heat until the Brussels sprouts are cooked through.

TO SERVE: Ladle 1 cup of broth into each serving bowl. Place some of the Brussels sprout salad in the center of each bowl. Slice the ends off the salmon and place on top.

Makes 6 servings

*A rotating mandolin is similar to a standard Japanese mandolin, but it's connected to a crank and produces curly-shaped strings of vegetables.

Skate Wing with Brown Butter Nage, Artichokes, Grilled Porcini, Capers, and Golden Raisins

ARTICHOKES

1 bottle Chardonnay

2 thyme sprigs

10 peppercorns

2 bay leaves

2 cups chicken stock (pg 166)

Kosher salt, to taste

1/4 cup extra virgin olive oil

2 artichokes, trimmed of coarse outer leaves, choke removed and cut into quarters, and held in a bowl of lemon water

NAGE

1/2 pound unsalted butter

1 lemon, juiced

1 egg yolk

1/4 cup chicken stock (pg 166)

Kosher salt and black pepper, to taste

PORCINI MUSHROOMS

4 porcini mushrooms

3 cups vegetable oil

2 thyme sprigs

2 chopped garlic cloves

1 chopped shallot

Kosher salt and black pepper, to taste

FOR THE ARTICHOKES: In a saucepan, combine the wine, thyme, peppercorns, and bay leaves. Reduce by half over medium heat. Add the chicken stock and salt, and simmer for 5 minutes more. Add the olive oil and quartered artichokes.

Cover with a non-dyed kitchen towel to keep the artichokes fully submerged. Simmer over low heat for 15 minutes or until the artichokes are tender and can be easily pierced with a knife. Remove the pot from the heat, and cool the artichokes in their cooking liquid until they come to room temperature. Reserve.

I love skate because of its unique, delicate texture. Here, I serve it with a simple sauce made by emulsifying egg yolks and chicken stock with browned butter. A careful emulsification allows for all the great flavors of brown butter without any of its greasiness. I like to garnish the plate with a mixture of raisins and capers for a delicate balance of sweetness and salt.

FOR THE NAGE: In a small saucepan, carefully brown the butter over medium-low heat for 10 minutes.

Combine the lemon juice, egg yolk, and chicken stock in a blender and mix well. With the motor running, slowly drizzle in the browned butter until the sauce thickens. Season to taste with salt, pepper, and if necessary, additional lemon juice. Transfer the sauce to a container and cover with plastic wrap—making sure that the plastic is touching the surface of the sauce. (This will prevent a skin from forming.)

FOR THE PORCINI: Preheat the oven to 275 degrees.

In an ovenproof pan, toss the porcini mushrooms with the vegetable oil, thyme, garlic, and shallots. Cover the pan with foil and roast the mixture for 1 hour. Cool to room temperature.

Recipe and ingredients continued on page 91.

SKATE

4 pieces of skate wing, about
6 ounces each
Kosher salt and black pepper, to taste
All-purpose flour, for dusting
2 tablespoons clarified butter

2 tablespoons capers
Vegetable oil, for frying
2 tablespoons golden raisins
16 tarragon leaves

Remove the mushrooms from the pan and cut in half. Transfer to a hot grill and char for 1 minute. Season to taste with salt and pepper.

FOR THE SKATE: Season the skate with salt and pepper. Dredge in flour and tap off the excess. Place in a hot sauté pan with a small amount of clarified butter. Cook for 3 minutes on each side or until golden brown.

TO COMPLETE: Drain the capers and rinse under cold running water. Dry thoroughly with a paper towel.

Pour vegetable oil into a large, heavy pot or a deep-fryer and heat to 350 degrees. Fry the capers until they split, about 1 minute. Remove the capers from the oil and drain on a paper towel.

Warm the artichokes and remove from the liquid.

TO SERVE: Ladle a small pool of nage in each shallow bowl. Arrange the mushrooms and artichokes on top. Garnish with fried capers, golden raisins, and tarragon leaves. Top with a piece of skate.

Makes 4 servings

Monkfish Paillard with Smoked Bacon, Lime, Cashews, and Arugula

APPLE SALAD

1/2 cup cashews

1 tablespoon fish sauce

1 teaspoon smoked paprika

1 pinch cayenne pepper

4 ounces smoked bacon

1/2 cup lychee juice

2 limes, juiced

1 sliced Granny Smith apple

1 cup arugula

BEURRE BLANC

3 chopped shallots

3 cups Chardonnay

1 bay leaf

2 thyme sprigs

1 tablespoon black pepper

1 tablespoon rice wine vinegar

1 pound unsalted butter

1 lemon, juiced

Kosher salt and black pepper, to taste

MONKFISH

8 ounces monkfish

Kosher salt and black pepper, to taste

All-purpose flour, for dusting

2 tablespoons clarified butter

FOR THE APPLE SALAD: Preheat the oven to 350 degrees.

Toss the cashews with the fish sauce, paprika, and cayenne pepper. Bake for 10 minutes and reserve.

Meanwhile, cut the bacon into 1/2-inch pieces and render in a medium sauté pan. Once the bacon is crispy, add the lychee juice and lime juice. Transfer to a mixing bowl and toss with the apple slices, arugula, and cashews.

FOR THE BEURRE BLANC: In a medium pot, combine the shallots, wine, bay leaf, thyme, pepper, and vinegar. Reduce to 3 tablespoons over medium-high heat. Lower the heat and slowly whisk in the butter and lemon juice. Season the sauce to taste with salt, pepper, and more lemon juice. Strain through a chinois and reserve in a warm part of the kitchen.

Monkfish is a sturdy fish that can stand up to more aggressive cooking methods—like being pounded out flat and seared in hot butter. It also lends to a savory, salty flavor combination—none more elegant than bacon, lychee juice, and apples with cayenne pepper and plenty of lime juice. The finishing touch is a drizzle of creamy beurre blanc.

FOR THE MONKFISH: Slice the monkfish into thin, 2-ounce portions. Place between 2 pieces of plastic wrap, and pound with a meat mallet until paper-thin.

Season the fish with salt and pepper. Dredge in flour, tapping off any excess. Sear the monkfish in a hot pan with 2 tablespoons of clarified butter until golden brown, about 1 minute on each side.

TO SERVE: Center some of the apple salad on each serving plate. Top with the monkfish and a drizzle of beurre blanc.

Makes 4 servings

Yellowtail Snapper with Littleneck Clams, Braised Leeks, and Parsley Vinaigrette

WHITE WINE NAGE

2 tablespoons unsalted butter
2 chopped celery ribs
1 chopped leek
1/2 chopped fennel bulb
2 chopped green garlic stems
1/2 chopped onion
2 cups Chardonnay
2 bay leaves
2 peppercorns

LITTLENECK CLAMS

12 littleneck clams, cleaned

PARSLEY PURÉE

2 bunches parsley, stems removed
2 tablespoons extra virgin olive oil
Kosher salt, to taste

BRAISED LEEKS

2 leeks, white parts only,
cut in half lengthwise
2 tablespoons unsalted butter
2 cups chicken stock (pg 166)
2 teaspoons kosher salt

SNAPPER

4 yellowtail snapper fillets, about
6 ounces each, skin on
Kosher salt, to taste
2 tablespoons clarified butter

3 tablespoons unsalted butter
Kosher salt and black pepper, to taste
1 tablespoon extra virgin olive oil

FOR THE WHITE WINE NAGE: In a pot, combine the butter, celery, leeks, fennel, green garlic, and onions. Cut out a circle of parchment paper, big enough to cover the pot. Cover the pot with the parchment paper and sweat the vegetables for 30 minutes over low heat. Add the wine, bay leaves, and peppercorns. Reduce by half, strain through a chinois, and reserve.

Return the nage to the pot, bring to a boil, and add the clams. Cover with a lid and continue to cook for 5 minutes or until the clamshells open. Remove the clams with a slotted spoon and set aside. Once cool, remove the meat from all but 4 shells and reserve separately. Strain the nage again and set aside.

FOR THE PARSLEY PURÉE: Blanch the parsley leaves in boiling, salted water for 15 seconds. Plunge into an ice water bath to stop the cooking process. Transfer the parsley to a blender and purée with 1 ice cube and 2 tablespoons of olive oil. Season to taste with salt.

FOR THE LEEKS: Place the leeks in a large pan with 2 tablespoons of butter and cover with a lid. Sweat over low heat for 10 minutes, or until they have released all their moisture. Add the chicken stock and salt. Continue to cook until the leeks are very tender, about 20 minutes. Remove from the chicken stock and reserve.

FOR THE SNAPPER: Season both sides of the snapper fillets with salt. Sear in a hot pan with 2 tablespoons of clarified butter. Lower the heat and continue to cook until the skin is crispy, about 5 minutes. Flip the fish and continue to cook 1 minute, or until just cooked through.

TO COMPLETE: Combine the parsley purée with white wine nage. Finish by whipping in the butter. Add the reserved clam meat, and season to taste with salt and pepper.

TO SERVE: Divide the nage into 4 serving bowls. Top with a row of braised leeks and a piece of snapper, placed skin-side-up. Garnish with a reserved clam and a drizzle of olive oil.

Makes 4 servings

There's virtually no limit to what you can do with snapper. It's a versatile fish that pairs well with a multitude of ingredients. Here, it's simply sautéed and served in a flavorful clam nage, a broth made by combining vibrant springtime ingredients like green garlic and parsley with fresh clams and white wine.

Eggplant Timbale with Olive Oil Emulsion, Crispy Fennel, and Roasted Tomatoes

ROASTED TOMATOES
4 Roma tomatoes
2 chopped garlic cloves
1 chopped rosemary sprig
2 chopped thyme sprigs
2 tablespoons extra virgin olive oil
Kosher salt and black pepper, to taste

EGGPLANT TIMBALE
1 tablespoon extra virgin olive oil
1 diced onion
4 minced garlic cloves
1 peeled eggplant, approximately 1/3 cut into 8 slices, the remaining diced
1 1/2 cups peeled and seeded tomatoes
2 tablespoons chopped rosemary
1 cup shredded Gruyère cheese
2 eggs
Vegetable oil, for frying

OLIVE OIL EMULSION
1/4 cup vegetable stock
2 egg yolks
1 tablespoon lemon juice
1 1/2 cups extra virgin olive oil
Kosher salt and black pepper, to taste

FOR THE ROASTED TOMATOES: Preheat the oven to 250 degrees.

Remove the stems from the tomatoes with a sharp knife. Cut each tomato in half from top to bottom. In a mixing bowl, toss with the chopped garlic, rosemary, thyme, olive oil, salt, and pepper. Place the tomatoes cut-side-up on a sheet pan and roast for 2 hours.

Here, a pouch of eggplant slices holds an assortment of savory Mediterranean ingredients like garlic, tomatoes, and more diced eggplant. The result is an unexpected burst of flavor when you cut into the package. I serve it over a pool of olive oil emulsion for a creamy finish.

FOR THE EGGPLANT TIMBALE: Turn up the oven to 350 degrees.

Over medium heat with 1 tablespoon of olive oil, sauté the onions, garlic, and diced eggplant until tender, about 4 minutes. Add the tomatoes and rosemary, and cook for 5 minutes more. Strain through a colander to remove any excess liquid. Cool to room temperature and set aside.

In a mixing bowl, toss the diced eggplant mixture with the cheese and eggs.

Pour vegetable oil into a large, heavy pot or a deep-fryer and heat to 350 degrees. Fry the eggplant slices until they become pliable, about 15 seconds per batch. Transfer to a paper towel and drain.

Line a 4-ounce ramekin with 2 eggplant slices (the eggplant should come up the sides of the ramekin). Press the center down until it touches the bottom of the dish. Repeat this process with the remaining eggplant slices and ramekins.

Carefully divide the diced eggplant mixture into each ramekin. Fold the excess eggplant slices over the top of the mixture to create a closed package.

Place the ramekins in a hotel pan or dish filled halfway with water. Cover with foil and bake for 30 minutes or until the eggplant mixture is firm. Carefully flip the ramekins upside down and shake the timbales onto a plate. Set aside.

Recipe and ingredients continued on page 98.

96

SPINACH

6 garlic cloves, peeled

2 diced shallots

1 tablespoon unsalted butter

1 quart curly spinach

Kosher salt and black pepper, to taste

FENNEL

1 fennel bulb

1 1/2 cups all-purpose flour

1/2 cup cornstarch

1 tablespoon baking powder

2 cups seltzer water

1 egg

Vegetable oil, for frying

Kosher salt and black pepper, to taste

FOR THE OLIVE OIL EMULSION: Bring the vegetable stock to a simmer in a small sauce pot.

Meanwhile, in a blender, combine the egg yolks and lemon juice. With the motor running, slowly add the hot vegetable stock (being careful not to let the eggs curdle). Mix on low speed until all the vegetable stock has been added.

Continue to blend as you slowly drizzle in the olive oil. When the oil is emulsified, season with salt and pepper. Reserve in a warm part of the kitchen.

FOR THE SPINACH: Slice the garlic on a mandolin. Transfer the garlic slices to a small pot of boiling water and blanch for 10 seconds. Strain and set aside.

Sauté the garlic and shallots in 1 tablespoon of butter over medium-low heat until fragrant, about 30 seconds. Add the spinach, and season with salt and pepper. Transfer the mixture to a paper towel and drain.

FOR THE FRIED FENNEL: Slice the fennel into paper-thin pieces on a mandolin.

Create a batter by combining the flour, cornstarch, baking powder, seltzer, and egg in a mixing bowl, being careful not to overwork the batter.

Pour vegetable oil into a large, heavy pot or deep-fryer and heat to 350 degrees. Dip the fennel in the batter, shaking off any excess. Fry for 1 minute or until golden brown and crispy. Transfer to a paper towel and drain. Season immediately with salt and pepper.

TO SERVE: Place a pool of olive oil emulsion in the center of each serving plate. Top with spinach and an eggplant timbale. Garnish with fennel and two roasted tomato halves.

Makes 4 servings

Halibut Cheeks with Green Garlic Gnudi, Wild Asparagus, and Truffle Vinaigrette

TRUFFLE VINAIGRETTE

1 egg

2 tablespoons red wine vinegar

1 tablespoon Dijon mustard

1 cup grape seed oil

2 tablespoons truffle oil

Kosher salt and black pepper, to taste

GNUDI

1 pound ricotta cheese

1 tablespoon clarified butter

1/4 cup green garlic

1 egg

1/2 cup pecorino

3/4 cup all-purpose flour

2 tablespoons extra virgin olive oil

WHITE ASPARAGUS

1/4 pound wild white asparagus

1 teaspoon diced shallots

1 tablespoon unsalted butter

Kosher salt and black pepper, to taste

HALIBUT

2 pounds halibut cheeks

Kosher salt and black pepper, to taste

All-purpose flour, for dusting

2 tablespoons clarified butter

1 tablespoon parsley oil (pg 169)

FOR THE TRUFFLE VINAIGRETTE: In a blender, combine the egg, vinegar, and Dijon mustard. With the motor running, slowly drizzle in the grape seed oil until the mixture is emulsified. Season with truffle oil, salt, and pepper. Set aside.

FOR THE GNUDI: Strain the ricotta in cheesecloth to remove any excess liquid.

In a sauté pan with the clarified butter, cook the green garlic until tender, about 5 minutes. Transfer the garlic to a container and cool in the refrigerator.

In a mixing bowl, combine the cooled garlic, ricotta cheese, egg, and pecorino. Gently fold in the flour, being careful not to overmix. Using 2 spoons, "quenelle" the gnudi. Transfer to salted, simmering water and cook for approximately 3 minutes. Strain and toss with 2 tablespoons of olive oil.

FOR THE ASPARAGUS: Blanch the asparagus in boiling water for 20 seconds.

Meanwhile, sweat the shallots in a sauté pan with 1 tablespoon of butter. Add the asparagus and season with salt and pepper. Reserve warm.

FOR THE HALIBUT: Season the halibut cheeks with salt and pepper. Lightly dust in flour, tapping off any excess.

Heat 2 tablespoons of clarified butter in a large skillet: the pan should be large enough to hold all the halibut without overcrowding. Over medium heat, sear the fish for 2 minutes on each side until golden brown.

TO SERVE: Place 3 gnudi in the bottom of each serving bowl. Top with a piece of halibut, sautéed asparagus, truffle vinaigrette, and drops of parsley oil.

Makes 4 servings

When halibut is at its peak, I love to utilize the entire fish—even the cheeks, which have a sweet, delicate flavor. Here, they're paired with pillow-soft gnudi, made with green garlic and coated in an earthy truffle vinaigrette.

Loup de Mer with Bay Scallops, Sage, Golden Raisins, Orange Reduction, and Caramelized Cauliflower

CAULIFLOWER

3 tablespoons unsalted butter

1 head of cauliflower: 1 cup diced into small pieces, the rest roughly chopped

2 tablespoons heavy cream, plus 3 tablespoons whipped to firm peaks

Kosher salt and white pepper, to taste

FRIED SAGE AND CAPERS

Vegetable oil, for frying

8 small sage leaves

3 tablespoons capers

LOUP DE MER

2 whole loup de mer, about 2 pounds each, filleted and skin left on

Kosher salt and white pepper, to taste

2 tablespoons clarified butter

ORANGE REDUCTION

2 cups Chardonnay

2 thinly sliced shallots

2 cups fresh-squeezed orange juice

1 cup chicken stock (pg 166)

1 cup unsalted butter

FOR THE SAUTÉED CAULIFLOWER: Heat a large sauté pan over high heat with 1 tablespoon of butter. Add the diced cauliflower and sauté until caramelized on all sides, adding more butter if the pan becomes too dry. After about 1 minute, season to taste with salt and pepper, and reserve warm.

FOR THE CAULIFLOWER PURÉE: Melt the remaining 2 tablespoons of butter in a large pan over low heat and add the roughly chopped cauliflower. Stir frequently until the cauliflower has released all of its moisture. After about 20 minutes, increase the heat and add the heavy cream (reserving the whipped cream for later use).

Once the mixture comes to a boil, transfer to a blender and purée on high until very smooth. Pass the cauliflower mixture through a tamis. Reserve warm.

FOR THE SAGE AND CAPERS: Pour vegetable oil into a large, heavy pot or deep-fryer and heat to 350 degrees. Fry the sage leaves until crispy, about 30 seconds. Remove the leaves and drain on a paper towel.

Rinse the capers under water and blot dry with a paper towel. Plunge in the hot vegetable oil and fry until crispy, about 30 seconds. Drain on a paper towel.

FOR THE LOUP DE MER: Cut each fillet into 3 equal portions and dry thoroughly with a paper towel. Season the skin side with salt and white pepper.

Heat 2 tablespoons of clarified butter in a sauté pan over medium heat. Place the fish in the pan, skin-side-down. Avoid letting the skin curl away from the pan by pressing the fish flat with a spoon. (If the skin curls too much, the fish will steam and may stick to the pan.) After about 3 minutes, or when the skin has crisped and the fish is almost cooked through, season the flesh side with salt and white pepper. Flip the fish over and cook about 20 seconds more. Remove from the pan and set aside.

Recipe and ingredients continued on page 104.

This is a wintertime meal that incorporates beautiful cold-weather ingredients: bay scallops, cauliflower, and tangy citrus. For balance, I speckle the plate with salty capers, sweet golden raisins, and loup de mer—a delicate white fish from the Mediterranean. If you can't find loup de mer, substitute any white, flaky fish such as striped sea bass or red snapper.

SCALLOPS

16 fresh bay scallops
Kosher salt and black pepper, to taste
1 tablespoon unsalted butter

1/4 cup golden raisins
1 orange, segmented
1 tablespoon sea salt

FOR THE ORANGE REDUCTION: In a pot over high heat, bring the wine and shallots to a simmer. Cook until reduced by half. Add the orange juice and reduce by half again. Pour in the chicken stock and reduce by half once more. Strain through a chinois and discard the solids. Return the liquid to the pot and bring to a simmer. Gently whip in the butter and reserve warm.

FOR THE SCALLOPS: Blot the scallops dry with a paper towel and season with salt and pepper. Sear on one side in a very hot sauté pan with 1 tablespoon of butter. After about 30 seconds, flip the scallops and cook 30 seconds more. Remove the scallops from the pan and reserve warm.

TO COMPLETE: Combine the whipped cream and puréed cauliflower with a hand blender. Season with salt and white pepper.

TO SERVE: Using a serving spoon, drag 1 tablespoon of cauliflower purée from one end of each serving plate to the other. Place 4 scallops on each plate, and garnish with fried sage leaves, golden raisins, fried capers, orange segments, and caramelized cauliflower. Top with loup de mer, skin-side-up, and season with sea salt. Spoon dots of the orange reduction around the fish and serve immediately.

Makes 4 servings

Crispy Tofu with Smoked Paprika, Arugula, and Grapefruit

PAPRIKA SAUCE

4 chopped shallots

3 tablespoons unsalted butter

1/4 cup smoked paprika

1/8 cup hot paprika

1 quart Chardonnay

1 bay leaf

1 quart vegetable stock

1 quart heavy cream

Kosher salt, to taste

TOFU

12 ounces firm tofu

All-purpose flour, for dredging

2 eggs whisked with 1 tablespoon milk, for egg wash

Panko crumbs, for dredging

2 tablespoons clarified butter

Kosher salt and black pepper, to taste

1 grapefruit, cut into segments

1 cup wild arugula

3 tablespoons lemon vinaigrette (pg 164)

3 tablespoons parsley oil (pg 169), in a squeeze bottle

FOR THE PAPRIKA SAUCE: In a saucepan, sweat the shallots in 1 tablespoon of butter until translucent. Add the smoked and hot paprikas, and continue to cook until fragrant, about 2 minutes. Add the wine and bay leaf. Reduce by half, about 5 minutes. Add the vegetable stock and reduce by half again. Pour in the heavy cream and reduce by half once more. Strain the sauce through a chinois and season with salt. Set aside.

I could almost drink the sauce in this dish as a soup; it's a spicy, velvety reduction made from hot and smoked paprikas, simmered in white wine and cream. To highlight its richness, I spoon the sauce over tofu, pan-fried simply in panko crumbs and topped with grapefruit segments. Every bite is a little spicy, a little smoky, and a little tangy.

FOR THE TOFU: Slice the tofu into 4 pieces. Prepare to bread by placing the flour, whipped eggs, and panko crumbs in 3 separate, shallow bowls. Coat the tofu first in flour, tapping off the excess. Transfer to the egg wash and coat evenly. Finish by rolling in panko crumbs.

Heat 2 tablespoons of clarified butter in a medium-hot sauté pan, and cook the tofu about 3 minutes on each side. Drain any excess butter, and season the tofu with salt and pepper.

TO COMPLETE: In a sauce pot, bring the paprika sauce to a simmer and whisk in the remaining 2 tablespoons of butter. Check for seasoning.

Toss the grapefruit and arugula with lemon vinaigrette.

TO SERVE: Ladle a pool of paprika sauce in the center of each serving plate. Place the tofu on top, and garnish with a handful of arugula, grapefruit segments, and dot with parsley oil.

Makes 4 servings

Seared Duck with Foie Gras Flan, Pickled Plums, Duck Jus, Sweet Corn Fritters, and Dried Corn

FOIE GRAS FLAN

3 1/2 ounces foie gras

2 eggs, plus 2 egg yolks

1 teaspoon kosher salt

1 cup heavy cream

Kosher salt and black pepper, to taste

PICKLED PLUMS

2 plums, sliced into 12 wedges

3/4 cup sugar

1 cup rice wine vinegar

2 star anise

2 tablespoons black peppercorns

CORN FRITTERS

6 ears of corn, still in husks

4 1/2 cups all-purpose flour

3 tablespoons baking powder

3 tablespoons sugar

1 tablespoon kosher salt

1/2 teaspoon cayenne pepper

1 teaspoon black pepper

1/4 cup minced chives

3 cups ice water

Vegetable oil, for frying

FOR THE FLAN: Preheat the oven to 350 degrees.

In a food processor, purée the foie gras, eggs, egg yolks, and salt. With the motor running, drizzle in the cream. Season with salt and pepper. Pass the mixture through a tamis.

Divide the custard into 4 greased 3-ounce ramekins. Set the ramekins in a hotel pan or a dish filled with 2 inches of water. Cover with foil and bake for 20 minutes or until the custard is set.

FOR THE PLUMS: Place the sliced plums in a bowl. Combine the sugar, vinegar, star anise, and peppercorns in a small pot over high heat. When the liquid comes to a simmer, pour over the plums. Cover with plastic wrap and set aside.

Duck is even more luxurious when paired with foie gras flan, but it needs an acidic component to cut through its richness. Here, I use pickled plums—though you could substitute another fruit like persimmons if they're available. To finish, I love the unexpected quality that comes from crispy corn fritters—fried simply in oil and topped with a spoonful of duck jus.

FOR THE CORN FRITTERS: Grill the ears of corn—while still in their husks—for 10 minutes or until slightly charred. Peel away the husks and remove the silks. Cut the corn off the cobs with a sharp knife, and transfer to a large mixing bowl.

Add the flour, baking powder, sugar, salt, cayenne, black pepper, and chives. Pour in the ice water, little by little, creating a thick batter and being careful not to overmix. Adjust the consistency of the dough by adding more flour if necessary.

Using a small scoop, make a series of 1-ounce dough balls.

Recipe and ingredients continued on the page 110.

Pour vegetable oil into a large, heavy pot or a deep-fryer and heat to 350 degrees. Fry the dough in batches for about 3 minutes or until cooked through and golden brown.

FOR THE DUCK JUS: With a sharp knife, separate the duck breast, legs, and thighs. Chop each duck carcass into about large 5 pieces. Reserve the legs and thighs for another use, and refrigerate the breasts until ready to use.

Heat 2 tablespoons of vegetable oil in a large sauté pan over medium heat. Add the bones and sauté until dark brown on all sides, about 20 minutes. Add the chopped carrots, celery, and onions, and cook until caramelized, about 5 minutes more. Pour in the wine and gently simmer until reduced by half. Add the bay leaves and chicken stock, and continue to simmer for 3 hours.

Strain the stock through a chinois and discard the solids. Transfer the liquid back to the pot, and reduce over medium heat until it coats the back of a spoon.

DUCK

2 ducks, 5 pounds each
2 tablespoons vegetable oil
1 chopped carrot
1 chopped celery rib
1/2 chopped onion
1 quart Pinot Noir
2 bay leaves
1 gallon chicken stock (pg 166)
Kosher salt and black pepper, to taste

1/4 cup dried corn

FOR THE SEARED DUCK: Season the duck breasts with salt and pepper. Place them skin-side-down in a room temperature cast-iron pan. Heat the pan over medium-low heat, and cook the duck until the skin is crispy, about 10 minutes.

Flip the duck and turn the heat to high. Continue to cook for about 2 minutes or until medium rare. Remove the pan from heat, and let the duck rest for 5 minutes before slicing into 1-inch pieces.

TO SERVE: Place the flan in the center of each serving plate. Fan the duck slices around the flan, and top with pickled plums, a corn fritter, dried corn, and a spoonful of duck jus.

Makes 4 servings

Braised Beef Cheeks with Spinach Gnudi, Shimeji Mushrooms, and Roasted Tomatoes

BEEF CHEEKS

1 pound beef cheeks, cleaned

Kosher salt, to taste

2 tablespoons clarified butter

1/4 cup soy sauce

1/2 cinnamon stick

1 star anise

3 thyme sprigs

4 garlic cloves

1 tablespoon black peppercorns

1 tablespoon honey

1/4 cup dry sherry

5 diced scallions

1 tablespoon sliced ginger

1 tablespoon Chinese black vinegar

1 quart chicken stock (pg 166)

ROASTED TOMATOES

4 Roma tomatoes

2 chopped garlic cloves

1 chopped rosemary sprig

2 chopped thyme sprigs

2 tablespoons extra virgin olive oil

Kosher salt and black pepper, to taste

FOR THE BEEF CHEEKS: Preheat the oven to 300 degrees.

Season the beef cheeks with salt. In clarified butter, sear the meat over high heat in a large Dutch oven or oven-ready pot. After 5 minutes, flip the beef and brown on the other side, about 5 minutes more.

Add the soy sauce, cinnamon, star anise, thyme, garlic, peppercorns, honey, sherry, scallions, ginger, vinegar, and chicken stock. Bring the mixture to a gentle simmer. Cover the pot with foil, and braise in the oven for 3 hours.

Remove the beef cheeks and set aside. Strain the sauce and return to the pot. Continue to simmer until intensified in flavor. Return the beef cheeks to the pot and reserve warm.

FOR THE ROASTED TOMATOES: Reduce the oven to 250 degrees.

Remove the stems from the tomatoes with a sharp knife. Cut each tomato in half from top to bottom. In a mixing bowl, toss with the chopped garlic, rosemary, thyme, olive oil, salt, and pepper. Place the tomatoes cut-side-up on a sheet pan and roast for 2 hours.

This is meat and potatoes done my way—beef cheeks infused with big Asian flavors and soft spinach gnudi. Make sure to get a nice sear on both sides of the meat before adding the braising liquid and simmering until tender. Gnudi, which are lighter, fluffier versions of gnocchi, are also delicious with wild ramps in the early spring.

FOR THE GNUDI: Blanch the spinach for 10 seconds in boiling water, then transfer to an ice water bath. When cool, squeeze the spinach dry and chop very fine. Set aside.

Recipe and ingredients continued on page 113.

GNUDI

1 cup spinach

1 cup ricotta cheese

1 egg

1/2 cup pecorino cheese

Kosher salt and black pepper, to taste

3/4 cup all-purpose flour

6 roasted garlic cloves (pg 167)

1/4 cup water

1/2 pound unsalted butter

SHIMEJI MUSHROOMS

1/2 cup all-purpose flour

1/2 cup cornstarch

1 teaspoon baking powder

1 teaspoon baking soda

1 egg

2/3 cup seltzer water

Vegetable oil, for frying

1 cup shimeji mushrooms

Purple potato chips (pg 168)

Strain the ricotta through a chinois to remove any excess liquid, and transfer to a mixing bowl. Add the chopped spinach, egg, pecorino, salt, and pepper. Gently fold in the flour with a rubber spatula—being careful not to overwork the dough. Add more flour as necessary to achieve a firm consistency.

Using an ice cream scoop, make a series of dough balls and transfer to a pot of salted, boiling water. Cook for 3 minutes and strain.

Bring the roasted garlic and water to a boil in a medium pot. After 1 minute, reduce to a simmer and gently whip in the cold butter. Keep the temperature of the butter mixture around 115 degrees, and continue to whisk until emulsified. Strain the mixture and return to the pot. Season with salt and toss with the gnudi. Reserve warm.

FOR THE SHIMEJI MUSHROOMS: In a mixing bowl, combine the flour, cornstarch, baking powder, baking soda, egg, and seltzer water. Chill in the refrigerator until ready to use.

Pour vegetable oil into a large, heavy pot or a deep-fryer and heat to 350 degrees. Dip the shimeji mushrooms in the batter, shaking off any excess. Transfer to the hot oil, and fry for 2 minutes or until golden brown and crispy. Drain on a paper towel.

TO SERVE: Place beef cheeks in each serving bowl with 4 ounces of broth. Top with an assortment of glazed gnudi, crispy mushrooms, roasted tomatoes, and purple potato chips.

Makes 4 servings

New York Strip with Bone Marrow Persillade and Périgueux Sauce

MARROW PERSILLADE

3 pounds veal femur bones,
cut into 3-inch sections

1 tablespoon Dijon mustard

1 tablespoon minced garlic

1 tablespoon minced shallots

2 teaspoons minced thyme

1/2 bunch minced parsley

Kosher salt and black pepper, to taste

PÉRIGUEUX SAUCE

1 cup chopped shallots

1 1/2 cups shiitake mushrooms

2 tablespoons clarified butter

2 tablespoons peppercorns

1/4 bunch thyme

2 bay leaves

1/2 bunch parsley stems

1 quart Madeira wine

3 cups brandy

1 cup port wine

1/2 cup black truffle juice

1 gallon veal stock (pg 167)

2 ounces sliced truffles

Black truffle oil, to taste

Kosher salt, to taste

2 ounces truffle butter

FOR THE MARROW PERSILLADE: Place the veal bones in ice water and allow them to soak for 2 hours. (This step will firm the marrow and remove any excess blood.)

Use your index finger to push the marrow out of the bones, being careful not to puncture it in the process. Dice the marrow into 1/2-inch pieces, and transfer to a mixing bowl. Add the mustard, garlic, shallots, thyme, parsley, salt, and pepper, and stir to combine. Set aside.

This is a deeply flavored strip steak, cooked in clarified butter for three hours at 125 degrees until perfectly medium rare. In the end, I like to sear it for color and deglaze the pan with soy sauce, imparting a lingering sense of umami. The Périgueux sauce is a truly decadent mixture of Madeira wine, veal demi-glace and truffles.

FOR THE PÉRIGUEUX SAUCE: In a pan over low heat, sweat the shallots and mushrooms in 2 tablespoons of clarified butter for 5 minutes. Add the peppercorns, thyme, bay leaves, and parsley stems, and continue to cook for 2 minutes.

Pour in the Madeira, brandy, port, and truffle juice, and reduce by half. Add the veal stock and reduce over low heat until the sauce coats the back of a spoon.

Strain the sauce through a chinois and return the liquid to the pot. Add the truffles and truffle oil. Check for seasoning and add salt if necessary.

FOR THE STEAKS: Fill a large pot or immersion circulator with clarified butter and heat to 125 degrees.

Recipe and ingredients continued on page 116.

STEAKS

1 quart clarified butter

6 New York strip steaks,
about 8 ounces each

Kosher salt and black pepper, to taste

2 tablespoons shiitake
mushroom powder

2 tablespoons smoked paprika

3 ounces soy sauce

Plunge the steaks in the butter and cook for 3 hours, being sure to keep the temperature of the butter around 125 degrees.

Transfer the steaks to a paper towel, and season with salt, pepper, shiitake mushroom powder, and smoked paprika.

Move the steaks to a hot pan, and sear until caramelized on one side, about 2 minutes. Flip the steaks and continue to brown, about 2 minutes more. Remove the pan from heat and deglaze with 3 ounces of soy sauce.

TO COMPLETE: Heat 12 ounces of Périgueux sauce in a pot and season with salt. Whisk in 2 ounces of truffle butter.

TO SERVE: Place the steaks on a sheet pan and top with 3 ounces of the marrow mixture. Broil until the marrow is hot, about 1 minute. Transfer the steaks to each serving plate, and serve with the Périgueux truffle sauce.

Makes 6 servings, with leftover Périgueux sauce

Roasted Lamb Loin with Carrot Ginger Purée, Matignon, Lemon Churro, and Madeira Sauce

CARROT PURÉE

2 thinly sliced carrots

1/2 cup candied ginger

3 tablespoons unsalted butter

2 tablespoons verjus

1/2 cup water

Kosher salt and black pepper, to taste

MADEIRA SAUCE

2 cups Madeira wine

3 peppercorns

1 chopped garlic clove

1 clove

3 chopped shallots

1-inch piece cinnamon

3 cups lamb stock

CHURRO

1 cup water

4 ounces unsalted butter

4 ounces all-purpose flour

3 eggs

Kosher salt, to taste

2 lemons, zested

Vegetable oil, for frying

FOR THE CARROT PURÉE: Combine the carrots, ginger, butter, verjus, and water in a pot.

Cover the pot partially with a lid, leaving room for steam to escape. Cook the carrots over medium heat until tender, about 15 minutes.

Transfer the carrot mixture to a blender and purée on high until smooth. Season with salt and pepper.

FOR THE MADEIRA SAUCE: In a pot, cook the Madeira, peppercorns, garlic, clove, shallots, and cinnamon until reduced by three-fourths. Add the lamb stock and reduce to 1 cup. Strain the sauce and reserve.

When you slowly cook onions, carrots, and celery in olive oil, they become intensely aromatic. I use the mixture as a filling for Swiss chard leaves, which I roll into tight, 2-inch cylinders. They work really well with lamb, which we smother in Dijon mustard and rosemary before browning and roasting in the oven.

FOR THE CHURRO: In a pot, cook the water and butter over low heat. When the butter is dissolved, add the flour and cook gently until the dough starts to pull away from the sides of the pot.

Transfer the dough to a mixing bowl and add the eggs, one at a time, making sure to incorporate each one before adding the next. Season with salt and lemon zest. Transfer the mixture to a pastry bag with a small star tip. Reserve.

FOR THE MATIGNON: Blanch the Swiss chard in boiling water until the leaves are tender, about 1 minute. Transfer to an ice water bath to stop the cooking process. Drain the water and set the Swiss chard aside.

Heat the olive oil over low heat, and add the onions, carrots, and celery.

Recipe and ingredients continued on page 120.

Cook until the vegetables are tender, about 10 minutes. Add the garlic and thyme and cook for 5 minutes more. Allow the mixture to cool.

Lay out 4 pieces of Swiss chard, stacked 2 leaves high. Season with salt and pepper.

Using a slotted spoon, spread a layer of vegetables in the center of each piece of Swiss chard. Fold each leaf in half, pushing the stuffing toward the closed side. Roll each leaf into a tight cylinder. (Make sure to tuck the left and right ends in before securing.) Roll each cylinder in plastic wrap to keep tight.

FOR THE LAMB: Preheat the oven to 400 degrees.

Remove the silver skin from the lamb loins with a sharp knife. Season the loins with salt and pepper.

Heat 2 tablespoons of clarified butter in a sauté pan over medium heat. Brown the lamb loins on all sides, about 4 minutes total. Remove from the heat, and coat in Dijon mustard, rosemary, and thyme.

Transfer the lamb to a roasting rack and cook in the oven for 4 minutes. Let the meat rest for 5 minutes before slicing into 1/2-inch pieces.

TO COMPLETE: Pour vegetable oil into a large, heavy pot or a deep-fryer and heat to 350 degrees. Pipe a 4-inch cylinder of churro dough into the fryer. Cook until the dough turns golden brown. Transfer to a paper towel and season with salt.

Place each matignon in a large pot of simmering water. Cook for 5 minutes or until just warmed through. Slice off the ends and remove the plastic wrap.

TO SERVE: Place a matignon on one end of each serving plate. Place 3 tablespoons of warm carrot purée on one side of the plate and drag to the other end. Fan the lamb over the carrot purée and top with a fried churro. Spoon some of the Madeira sauce next to the lamb and serve immediately.

Makes 4 servings

MATIGNON

8 large Swiss chard leaves, stems removed

1/2 cup extra virgin olive oil

1 diced onion

2 diced carrots

2 diced celery ribs

3 chopped garlic cloves

3 minced thyme sprigs

Kosher salt and black pepper, to taste

LAMB

4 lamb loins

Kosher salt and black pepper, to taste

2 tablespoons clarified butter

2 tablespoons Dijon mustard

2 tablespoons chopped rosemary

2 tablespoons chopped thyme

Rabbit with Serrano Ham, Foie Gras, Polenta Galette, White Asparagus, and Raspberries

RABBIT

3 fryer rabbits, 4 pounds each
1/2 cup heavy cream
Kosher salt and black pepper, to taste
4 ounces julienned Serrano ham
5 ounces diced foie gras

2 cups curly spinach, stems removed
Kosher salt and black pepper, to taste
All-purpose flour, for dredging
2 tablespoons clarified butter

1 1/2 cups all-purpose flour
1/2 cup cornstarch
1 tablespoon baking powder
2 cups seltzer water
1 egg
Vegetable oil, for frying

Kosher salt and black pepper, to taste
2 tablespoons clarified butter

RABBIT JUS

1 chopped fennel bulb
4 chopped celery ribs
2 chopped leeks
2 cups raspberry vinegar
1/2 cup sugar
1 gallon chicken stock (pg 166)

TO PREPARE THE RABBIT: Debone the rabbits with a sharp knife: separating the front legs, hindquarters, loins, tenderloins, and belly meat. Separate the thighs from the hind legs. Combine the meat from the hind legs, bellies, and tenderloins, transfer to a bowl, and chill in the freezer until very cold. Reserve the carcasses for the jus, and the thighs, loins, and front legs for the final preparation.

FOR THE FORCEMEAT: Remove the meat from the freezer and grind in a meat grinder. Transfer to a mixing bowl and place inside another bowl of ice water. (The colder the rabbit meat remains, the better it will emulsify in the following steps.) Place the bowls in the freezer and chill for 5 minutes.

Once ice cold, transfer the rabbit meat to a food processor. With the motor running, drizzle in the cream, being careful not to overprocess. Season with salt and pepper.

Transfer the meat to a bowl and place over ice water again. Pass the forcemeat through a tamis. Fold in the ham and foie gras. Set aside.

Serving rabbit three ways is an ambitious undertaking—but one that's incredibly rewarding on the plate. After pounding out the thighs and lining them with spinach, I stuff them with forcemeat made from a combination of foie gras and Serrano ham. Rolled into vibrant pinwheels of color, the thighs are served alongside seared tenderloin and crispy fried legs.

FOR THE THIGHS: Blanch the spinach in boiling, salted water for 10 seconds. Transfer to an ice bath to cool. Strain the ice water and set aside.

Use a meat mallet to gently pound the thighs into 3/4-inch-thick pieces.

Season with salt and pepper. Place a thin layer of spinach over the top of each thigh. Top with another layer of rabbit forcemeat.

Recipe and ingredients continued on page 123.

POLENTA GALETTE

1 pint whole milk

1 pint chicken stock (pg 166)

2 ounces unsalted butter

13 ounces polenta

2 ounces Parmigiano-Reggiano

2 teaspoons chopped thyme

Kosher salt and black pepper, to taste

2 tablespoons clarified butter

18 white asparagus spears, peeled
and cut 3 inches from the bottom

1 tablespoon unsalted butter, melted

1 pint of fresh raspberries

1/4 cup micro tatsoi

Roll the thighs into cylinders, being careful not to lose any filling. Wrap the thighs in plastic wrap, and twist the ends into tight knots. If possible, seal the plastic-wrapped rabbit in a vacuum pack.

Pour 1 gallon of water into a large pot or immersion circulator, and heat to 160 degrees. Plunge the thighs into the water and cook for 30 minutes or until the internal temperature of the rabbit reaches 150 degrees. Remove the thighs and shock in an ice water bath.

Remove the plastic and check the rabbit for seasoning. Roll the thighs in dredging flour and tap off any excess. In a hot sauté pan with 2 tablespoons of clarified butter, sear the rabbit until golden brown and warmed through.

FOR THE RABBIT LEGS: Create a batter by combining the flour, cornstarch, baking powder, seltzer water, and egg in a large mixing bowl.

Pour vegetable oil into a large, heavy pot or a deep-fryer and heat to 350 degrees. Dip the rabbit legs in the batter and fry for 2 minutes or until golden brown.

FOR THE RABBIT LOIN: Season the rabbit loin with salt and pepper. Heat 2 tablespoons of clarified butter in a sauté pan over high heat. Sear the rabbit for 1 minute and flip. Continue to cook until the rabbit is medium, about 1 minute.

FOR THE RABBIT JUS: Sear the reserved rabbit carcasses in a large pot until the bones turn golden brown. Add the vegetables and cook until lightly caramelized. Pour in the raspberry vinegar and sugar. Cook until reduced by half. Add the chicken stock and simmer until reduced by half again. Strain the sauce through a chinois and return to the pot. Reduce over low heat until the sauce coats the back of a spoon.

FOR THE POLENTA: Combine the milk, chicken stock, and butter in a large pot and bring to a boil. Whisk in the polenta and reduce to a simmer. Stir the polenta for about 10 minutes or until it starts to pull away from the sides of the pot. Fold in the cheese, thyme, salt, and pepper.

Using a spatula, spread the polenta evenly onto a sheet pan. Place the sheet pan in the refrigerator and cool.

Recipe continued on page 124.

Cut the polenta into circles with a 2-inch ring cutter. Heat 2 tablespoons of clarified butter in a sauté pan over high heat. Sear the polenta for 2 minutes or until golden brown on both sides.

TO COMPLETE: Simmer the asparagus in salted water until tender, about 3 minutes. Transfer to a bowl of ice water to stop the cooking process. In a sauté pan over low heat, reheat the asparagus with 1 tablespoon of melted butter. Remove the ends of the rabbit thighs with a sharp knife to expose the filling.

TO SERVE: Place a polenta galette in the center of each serving plate and top with 3 pieces of asparagus. Place a thigh and a leg next to the polenta. Slice a rabbit loin in half and place over the asparagus. Garnish with raspberries, micro tatsoi, and a drizzle of the rabbit jus.

Makes 6 servings

Roasted Fallow Venison with Spiced Cranberries, Salsify, Almonds, and Juniper Berry Sauce

CRANBERRY SAUCE

1 12-ounce bag cranberries

1 quart water

5 cardamom pods

1 1/2 vanilla beans, split

2 cups sugar

4 1/2 teaspoons agar powder

6 gelatin sheets, soaked
in cold water to soften

SALSIFY

3 peeled and julienned salsify roots

3 cups chicken stock (pg 166)

1 bay leaf

2 thyme sprigs

Kosher salt and black pepper, to taste

1 cup all-purpose flour

2 eggs, whisked for egg wash

2 cups ground almonds

Vegetable oil, for frying

JUNIPER BERRY SAUCE

2 cups ruby port wine

4 thyme sprigs

3 tablespoons juniper berries

1 cup sliced button mushrooms

1 quart veal stock (pg 167)

FOR THE CRANBERRY SAUCE: In a large pot, stew the cranberries, water, cardamom, vanilla beans, and sugar until the cranberries are tender, about 20 minutes. Remove the vanilla beans and purée the mixture in a blender until smooth. Strain through a chinois.

Transfer 1 quart of the liquid back to the pot. Add the agar powder. Simmer over low heat for 3 minutes, stirring constantly.

Take the pot off the heat. Once the cranberries have cooled slightly, add the gelatin sheets and mix until completely dissolved. Strain through a chinois and reserve.

Line the inside of four 2-inch ring molds with acetate. Wrap the bottom of the ring molds with plastic wrap, and secure tightly by twisting the ends into tight knots. Repeat this process 3 more times to ensure that the plastic will remain intact when hot liquid is poured inside.

Gently pour the cranberry mixture into the molds. Place the molds in the refrigerator and set for at least 4 hours.

It's hard to think of special meals around the holidays without thinking of cranberries. I like to make mine from scratch, infusing subtle flavors of vanilla and cardamom. They're great with roasted turkey—or in this case, venison with a touch of juniper berry sauce.

FOR THE SALSIFY: Place the salsify in a pot with the chicken stock, bay leaf, and thyme. Season lightly with salt and pepper. Bring the mixture to a simmer and cook until the salsify is tender, about 5 minutes. Allow the salsify to cool in the stock until room temperature.

Place the flour, egg wash, and almonds into three separate shallow bowls. Remove the salsify from the chicken stock and coat in flour, tapping off any excess. Transfer to the egg wash and coat evenly. Roll in the almonds and reserve until ready to serve.

Recipe and ingredients continued on page 128.

VENISON

2 venison loins, 10 ounces each

Kosher salt and black pepper, to taste

2 tablespoons Ras el Hanout, ground into a powder

2 tablespoons clarified butter

JUNIPER BERRY SAUCE: Combine the port wine, thyme, 2 tablespoons juniper berries, and mushrooms in a pot and bring to a simmer. Cook until reduced by half. Add the veal stock and reduce by half again. Crack the remaining juniper berries with the back of a knife and add to the sauce. Steep for 10 minutes and strain.

FOR THE VENISON: Season the venison with salt, pepper, and Ras el Hanout.

Heat 2 tablespoons of clarified butter in a large sauté pan over medium heat. Add the venison and cook for 2 minutes or until caramelized on one side. To serve rare, flip the venison and cook about 2 minutes more. Remove from the pan and let rest for 5 minutes.

TO COMPLETE: Remove the cranberries from the molds, and place one in the center of each serving plate. Set aside until the cranberries come to room temperature.

Meanwhile, pour vegetable oil into a large, heavy pot or a deep-fryer and heat to 350 degrees. Add the almond-coated salsify and fry until golden brown, about 2 minutes per batch.

TO SERVE: Slice the venison loin into 1-inch pieces and fan around the cranberries. Garnish with salsify and a drizzle of juniper berry sauce.

Makes 4 servings

Roasted Quail with Spiced Pumpkin Purée, Pepitas, Pomegranates, and Port Wine Hibiscus Reduction

PUMPKIN PURÉE

1 sugar pumpkin
2 tablespoons extra virgin olive oil
Kosher salt and white pepper, to taste
1 tablespoon Chinese five-spice
1/4 cup heavy cream

PEPITAS

1 tablespoon unsalted butter
1/2 cup pumpkin seeds
Kosher salt and black pepper, to taste

PORT WINE HIBISCUS REDUCTION

1 quart ruby port wine
1/2 cup dried hibiscus flowers
2 cups pomegranate juice

QUAIL

4 quails
Vegetable oil, for frying
1 1/2 cups all-purpose flour
1/2 cup cornstarch
1 tablespoon baking powder
1 egg
2 cups seltzer water
Kosher salt and black pepper, to taste
1 tablespoon clarified butter

2 tablespoons pomegranate seeds
1 small bunch of corn shoots

FOR THE PUMPKIN PURÉE: Preheat the oven to 300 degrees.

Chop the pumpkin into 8 equal slices and reserve the seeds.

Drizzle the pumpkin wedges with olive oil, and season with salt and white pepper. Transfer to a sheet pan, skin-side-down, and cover with foil. Roast in the oven for 1 hour or until tender.

Peel the skin from the flesh and pass the pumpkin through a tamis. Transfer the flesh to a pot, and add the Chinese five-spice and heavy cream. Whip with an immersion blender until incorporated. Reserve warm.

FOR THE PEPITAS: Melt the butter in a sauté pan and add the reserved pumpkin seeds. Toast for 2 minutes on low heat or until the seeds are fragrant. Season with salt and pepper.

Quails are fun to eat, but only if they're properly manicured. That's because careful butchery makes it possible to apply different cooking methods to different parts of the bird. Here, the legs and thighs are battered and deep-fried, while the breasts are seared and served medium. Paired with a sweet pumpkin purée and a tart port reduction, it's a great, balanced fall dish.

FOR THE HIBISCUS REDUCTION: Place the port wine and hibiscus flowers in a pot, and gently simmer until reduced by half, about 10 minutes. Add the pomegranate juice and cook until the mixture coats the back of a spoon. Strain and reserve at room temperature.

FOR THE QUAIL: Debone the quails, leaving the wings attached to the breasts. French the wings by pulling the skin back from the top of the joint and exposing the bone.

Recipe continued on page 131.

Remove the quail legs with the thighs still attached. Cut out the leg joints and French the bones—pulling the skin away from the top of the joints. Use pliers to remove the exposed leg tendons. Remove the bone from the thighs. Gently curl the thigh meat around the base of the leg bone and secure with a skewer. Reserve.

Pour vegetable oil into a large, heavy pot or a deep-fryer and heat to 350 degrees.

Create a batter by combining the flour, cornstarch, baking powder, egg, and seltzer water in a mixing bowl.

Coat the quail leg and thigh in batter, and transfer to the hot vegetable oil. Fry for 1 minute or until crispy and golden brown. Drain on a paper towel, remove skewer, and season immediately with salt.

Season the quail breast with salt and pepper. Sear in a hot sauté pan with 1 tablespoon of clarified butter. Cook for 1 minute on each side or until medium.

TO SERVE: Pull a spoonful of pumpkin purée from one side of each plate to the other. Randomly place the quail legs and breast on top of the pumpkin purée. Garnish with pepitas, pomegranate seeds, and corn shoots. Finish with a drizzle of port wine hibiscus reduction.

Makes 4 servings

Grilled Filet Mignon with Oyster Mushroom Gratinée

GRATINÉE

2 cups sliced oyster mushrooms

2 cups sliced shiitake mushrooms

2 tablespoons unsalted butter

1 teaspoon chopped garlic

3 tablespoons chopped shallots

1/4 cup Dry Sack Sherry

1 3/4 cups heavy cream

1/2 cup veal demi-glace

3 tablespoons cornstarch slurry (equal parts cornstarch and cold water combined)

HERB CRUST

3 tablespoons minced basil

3 tablespoons minced thyme

1/2 cup grated Parmigiano-Reggiano

1/2 cup grated Gruyère

1/2 cup breadcrumbs

RED WINE SAUCE

1 quart Cabernet Sauvignon

1 pint Ruby Port

2 bay leaves

1 tablespoon peppercorns

1/2 pound thinly sliced shallots

1 cup mushroom stems

2 quarts chicken stock (pg 166)

Kosher salt, to taste

2 tablespoons unsalted butter

FILET MIGNON

4 pieces filet mignon, 8 ounces each

Kosher salt and black pepper, to taste

Extra virgin olive oil, for brushing

1/4 cup English peas

8 baby carrots

2 tablespoons extra virgin olive oil

Kosher salt and black pepper, to taste

FOR THE GRATINÉE: In a sauté pan over medium heat, cook the mushrooms in 2 tablespoons of butter for about 3 minutes. When caramelized, add the garlic and shallots, and continue to cook until soft and translucent. Remove the mushrooms from the pan and add the sherry, cream, and veal demi-glace. Add the cornstarch slurry and cook for 5 minutes. When the sauce thickens, after about 2 minutes, return the mushrooms to the pan and reserve.

FOR HERB BREADCRUMBS: In a mixing bowl, combine the herbs, cheeses, and breadcrumbs.

FOR THE RED WINE SAUCE: In a large pot, combine the first 6 ingredients. Cook over medium heat until reduced to 3 cups. Add the chicken stock and reduce until the sauce coats the back of a spoon.

Strain the liquid through a chinois and discard the solids. Check for seasoning, adding salt if necessary. Swirl in the butter and reserve warm.

What's great about this dish is that it's elegant enough for a special occasion but comforting enough for Sunday evening. When you reduce red wine with port and stock, it becomes rich and intensely flavored—perfect for smothering over a thick cut of filet mignon. I serve it over a rustic mushroom gratinée—which is almost like the casseroles I remember eating as a kid— but elevated with a generous hand of sherry and veal demi-glace.

FOR THE STEAK: Season each filet mignon generously with salt and pepper. Brush lightly with olive oil and place on a hot grill. Cook for 5 minutes on each side or until medium rare.

TO COMPLETE: In a pot of boiling salted water, blanch the peas and carrots separately until tender. Strain and toss the vegetables with olive oil. Season with salt and pepper.

Sprinkle the herb breadcrumbs over the mushrooms. Transfer the pan to the oven, and broil until golden brown.

TO SERVE: Place 1/2 cup of warm mushroom gratinée in the center of each serving plate. Top with a piece of grilled filet mignon, and garnish with peas and baby carrots. Finish with 3 tablespoons of red wine sauce.

Makes 4 servings

DESSERTS

Thanks to collaboration with Pastry Chef Megan Ketover, new dessert concepts are always in motion at Orchids at Palm Court. We banter back and forth. Snap pictures. Tear out articles. And though our dishes are wholly original, they're always rooted in the flavors that we craved as kids. Ice cream. Peanut butter. Hot fudge. So whether you're being served supremely moist chocolate cake or s'mores with gooey marshmallows, you're getting some of that nostalgia. And hopefully, you're punctuating a satisfying meal—and making room for even more brilliant memories.

S'mores with Warm Chocolate Custard

WHITE CHOCOLATE MARSHMALLOW

12 ounces corn syrup

15 sheets gelatin, bloomed in cold water

1 pound sugar

2 ounces water

1/2 teaspoon lemon juice

8 ounces white chocolate, melted

1 tablespoon unsalted butter, to coat

Powdered sugar, for dusting

CHOCOLATE CUSTARD

2 eggs

1/4 teaspoon kosher salt

3/4 cup sugar

2 tablespoons cornstarch

3 ounces dark chocolate

2 ounces unsalted butter

1 cup heavy cream

1/2 teaspoon vanilla extract

GRAHAM CRACKERS

2 1/2 cups pastry flour

1 cup dark brown sugar

1 teaspoon baking soda

3/4 teaspoon salt

8 ounces unsalted butter, cubed and cold

1/3 cup honey

2 ounces milk

2 tablespoons vanilla extract

FOR THE MARSHMALLOWS: In a small pot, warm the corn syrup and dissolve the gelatin. Transfer to stand-up mixer.

In a separate pot, combine the sugar, water, and lemon juice. Bring to a boil and cook to 243 degrees. Add to the corn syrup and mix on low speed. Turn the speed up to medium high, and whip until tripled in volume and room temperature. Pour in the white chocolate.

Line a rimmed quarter sheet pan with parchment paper and grease with unsalted butter. Pour the marshmallow mixture in the sheet pan and press firmly with a spatula. Set overnight.

Cut the marshmallows into 2-inch cubes. Toss in powdered sugar and set aside.

S'mores aren't just for smoky childhood campfires anymore—at Orchids at Palm Court, they're a sophisticated dessert course. We use a chocolate-baked custard that's rich and still warm from the oven—then top it with a homemade graham cracker, a perfectly charred marshmallow, and a scoop of ice cream.

FOR THE CHOCOLATE CUSTARD: Preheat the oven to 350 degrees. In a mixing bowl, whip the eggs and salt together. Sift in the sugar and cornstarch.

Combine the dark chocolate, butter, and heavy cream in a small pot, and melt over low heat. Slowly temper into the egg mixture and whisk until well incorporated. Stir in the vanilla extract. Divide the custard into six 4-ounce ramekins. Bake for approximately 20 minutes or until the centers are set.

FOR THE GRAHAM CRACKERS: Combine the dry ingredients in a mixing bowl. Cut in the cold butter and stir until it resembles cornmeal. Add the honey, milk, and vanilla extract. Mix until the dough comes together.

Recipe and ingredients continued on page 138.

GRAHAM CRACKER TUILES

1 ounce unsalted butter, cooked
over low heat until solids turn brown

1/3 cup simple syrup

YUZU CURD

4 eggs

1 cup sugar

3/4 cup yuzu juice

9 ounces unsalted butter, softened

6 scoops caramel ice cream (pg 148)

Roll the dough into a thin layer between two layers of parchment paper. Transfer to the refrigerator. Once cool, cut the dough into rectangles. Bake at 350 degrees for 7 to 10 minutes, or until light brown. Cool to room temperature and transfer a few of the graham crackers to a food processor. Process until the grahams break down into crumbs. Repeat until you have 1 cup of graham cracker crumbs.

FOR THE GRAHAM CRACKER TUILES: In a food processor, pulse the graham cracker crumbs and butter. Slowly add the simple syrup, and mix until a smooth paste forms. Using a spatula, spread the dough onto a rectangle stencil. Bake at 350 degrees for 7 minutes or until the crackers are firm and crispy.

FOR THE YUZU CURD: Whisk the eggs and sugar in a bowl. Heat the yuzu juice in a saucepan and temper into the egg mixture. Cook over a water bath until 185 degrees and thick. Whisk in the butter, 1 tablespoon at a time. Chill in the refrigerator.

TO COMPLETE: Caramelize the marshmallows with a cooking blowtorch. Warm the chocolate custard in the oven.

TO SERVE: Place chocolate custard on each serving plate and top with a caramelized marshmallow. Serve with a graham cracker tuile, a scoop of caramel ice cream, and 1 tablespoon of yuzu curd.

Makes 6 servings, with leftover marshmallows and graham crackers

Chocolate Bavarian with Milk Chocolate Biscuit and Marinated Blackberries

CHOCOLATE BAVARIAN CREAM

3/4 cup milk

1 quart plus 1/2 cup heavy cream

2 ounces sugar

1/4 cup egg yolks

4 ounces dark chocolate,
finely chopped

2 gelatin sheets, bloomed in cold water

MILK CHOCOLATE BISCUIT LAYER

5 ounces milk chocolate,
finely chopped

4 ounces unsalted butter, softened

4 eggs, yolks and whites separated

1 ounce glucose

2 ounces sugar

2 ounces cake flour, sifted

CHOCOLATE DENTELLE LACE COOKIE

1 cup almond flour

1/2 cup sugar

2 tablespoons cocoa powder,
Valrhona preferred

2 ounces milk

2 ounces corn syrup

4 ounces unsalted butter

FOR THE BAVARIAN CREAM: In a small pot, bring the milk, 1/2 cup of heavy cream, and sugar to a boil. In a mixing bowl, whisk the egg yolks until light in color. Gradually temper the warm milk mixture into the egg yolks.

Return the mixture to the pot, heat to 180 degrees, and mix constantly until it coats the back of a spoon. Remove from heat, add the chocolate, and whisk until smooth. Add the gelatin and stir to dissolve.

Set a mixing bowl on top of an ice water bath. Pour the chocolate into the bowl and cool to room temperature, stirring occasionally.

In a separate bowl, whip 1 quart of heavy cream to medium peaks, and fold into the chocolate mixture.

Divide the mixture into eight 3-inch molds, smooth out the top with a spatula, and freeze overnight.

We were honored when Orchids at Palm Court was selected to host the first dinner created for the Les Amis d'Escoffier Society. For the special occasion, I challenged Pastry Chef Megan Ketover to create a modern twist on a classic chocolate Bavarian. This rendition uses a unique set of garnishes— cinnamon-spiked blackberries and an elegant chocolate cookie.

FOR THE BISCUIT LAYER: Preheat the oven to 350 degrees.

In a mixing bowl set over a bowl of warm water, slowly melt the chocolate and butter. Then slowly whisk in the egg yolks and glucose.

In the bowl of a stand-up mixer, combine the egg whites and sugar. Whip to firm peaks. Fold in the cake flour and chocolate mixture.

Line a half sheet pan with parchment paper and spread the batter on top. Bake for 12 minutes or until light and firm. Remove from the oven and cool. Use a 3-inch ring mold to stamp out a series of biscuits. (This will serve as the base the dessert.)

Recipe and ingredients continued on page 141.

FEUILLETINE CRUMBLE

4 ounces milk chocolate, melted

8 ounces praline paste

8 ounces feuilletine

SPICED BLACKBERRIES

1/2 cup sugar

1/2 cup water

Pinch fresh-ground black pepper

1 star anise

1 cinnamon stick

1/4 teaspoon ginger

1 pint sliced blackberries

2 tablespoons chocolate sauce

FOR THE COOKIE: Keep the oven at 350 degrees.

In a food processor, mix the almond flour, sugar, and cocoa powder.

In a sauce pot, bring the milk, corn syrup, and butter to a boil. After 2 minutes, add the almond mixture. Remove from heat and cool to room temperature.

Scoop several teaspoon-sized balls onto a parchment-lined sheet pan. Bake for 10 minutes or until the cookies bubble and are slightly firm to the touch. (The cookies will continue to crisp as they cool.)

FOR THE FEUILLETINE CRUMBLES: In a mixing bowl, combine the melted chocolate and praline paste. Fold in the feuilletine and incorporate. Roll between 2 pieces of parchment paper into a 1/4-inch-thick layer. Refrigerate for 2 hours, and chop into crumbles.

FOR THE SPICED BLACKBERRIES: In a small pot, bring the sugar and water to a boil. Add the spices and steep for 10 minutes. Put the blackberries in a mixing bowl and pour the sugar mixture over the top. Marinate the berries for 20 minutes. Strain the liquid out, and set the berries aside.

TO SERVE: Paint a streak of chocolate sauce on each serving plate and top with a biscuit. Unmold the Bavarian creams and set one on each biscuit. Top with a cookie. Finish with a line of feuilletine crumbles and a few spiced blackberries.

Makes 8 servings

Chocolate Decadence

GANACHE

1 pound dark chocolate, finely chopped

12 ounces heavy cream

EXTRA DARK CHOCOLATE CAKE

2 cups sugar

1 1/2 cups all-purpose flour

1 cup extra dark cocoa powder

1 1/2 teaspoons baking powder

1 1/2 teaspoons baking soda

1 teaspoon kosher salt

2 eggs

1 cup milk

1/2 cup vegetable oil

2 teaspoons vanilla extract

1 cup boiling water

2-3 tablespoons heavy cream, as needed

8 edible gold leaves

1 pint raspberries

FOR THE GANACHE: Pour the chocolate in a mixing bowl. In a small pot, bring the heavy cream to a boil. Pour over the chopped chocolate. As the cream melts the chocolate, whisk to incorporate. Cover and store overnight at room temperature.

FOR THE CHOCOLATE CAKE: Preheat the oven to 350 degrees. Grease two 9-inch cake pans lined with parchment paper.

In a stand-up mixer, blend the sugar, flour, cocoa, baking powder, baking soda, and salt. Add the eggs, milk, oil, and vanilla extract. Beat on medium speed for 2 minutes. Gradually add the boiling water.

Pour the batter in the cake pans and spread into even layers. Bake for approximately 35 minutes, or until the cakes rise and spring back in the center. Cool before removing from the pans.

For decades, the Netherland Plaza has been known for this signature dessert—a towering, dense chocolate cake with loads of ganache. It's been handed down from chef to chef for generations—becoming so popular that we always have the ingredients on hand to satisfy special requests.

TO COMPLETE: Slice the cakes horizontally into half-inch layers. Spread each layer with a thick coating of ganache. Stack the layers on top of each other and coat the entire cake with another layer of ganache. Refrigerate until the outside of the cake is firm.

Transfer the cake to a wire rack. Heat the leftover ganache over a warm water bath, and thin with a small amount of cream. Pour the ganache over the cake to glaze. Pipe rosettes on top and garnish with gold leaves and raspberries.

Makes 8 servings

Old Kentucky Tomme with Bourbon Barrel Vanilla Sorghum, Lavash, and Honeycomb

2 1/2 cups all-purpose flour

1 teaspoon sugar

1 teaspoon kosher salt

2/3 cup water

2 egg whites, beaten

2 tablespoons unsalted butter, melted

2 tablespoons chopped shallots

1 tablespoon sea salt

8 ounces Old Kentucky Tomme

4 ounces honeycomb

2 black mission figs, halved

1 cup mizuna

1 tablespoon extra virgin olive oil

2 ounces Bourbon Barrel Foods bourbon vanilla sorghum

Preheat the oven to 400 degrees.

In a large bowl, combine the flour, sugar, and salt. Add the water, 1 egg white, and the melted butter. Mix until the dough stiffens, and knead for 5 minutes until smooth.

Roll the dough into a paper-thin sheet with a rolling pin. Brush with the remaining egg white. Sprinkle with diced shallots and sea salt. Cut into 2-inch rectangles and transfer to an ungreased sheet pan.

Bake for 10 to 12 minutes, or until the crackers are golden brown and the shallots are caramelized.

This composed cheese course highlights ingredients that are unique to the Ohio River Valley: Old Kentucky Tomme—a fantastic aged goat cheese from Indiana—and vanilla-infused sorghum from Bourbon Barrel Foods in Kentucky. The result is an ideal sweet and savory combination—complete with a honeycomb made from the Netherland Plaza beehive.

TO SERVE: Place 2 ounces of cheese on each serving plate. Top with a honeycomb and a half of a black mission fig. Divide the mizuna onto each plate and drizzle with olive oil. Center a lavash cracker on the cheese and surround with a line of bourbon vanilla sorghum.

Makes 4 servings

Crème Brûlée with Seasonal Fruit

3 cups heavy cream

5 ounces sugar

1 vanilla bean, split

2 pink peppercorns

3/4 cup egg yolks

1/2 cup turbinado sugar

Seasonal fruit: Champagne grapes, Concord grapes, golden raspberries, cape gooseberries, rambutans

Preheat the oven to 300 degrees.

In a pot, bring the heavy cream, sugar, vanilla bean, and pink peppercorns to a boil.

In a mixing bowl, whisk the egg yolks vigorously until light in color. Slowly temper the cream mixture into the eggs, and whisk to combine. Remove the vanilla bean and strain through a chinois.

Crème brûlée is a classic dessert, and it's widely popular all over North America and Europe. To distinguish ours, we rely on craftsman-like technique and a unique garnish—an assortment of seasonal fruit. From Champagne grapes and rambutans to golden raspberries and cape gooseberries, our fruit is always at the height of seasonal perfection.

Pour 4 ounces of custard into each ramekin. Transfer the ramekins to an ovenproof dish or a hotel pan filled with 2 inches of water. Bake for 30 minutes or until the crème brûlée is set in the center.*

Cool to room temperature. Sprinkle the turbinado sugar around the top of the baked custards. Using a small torch, gently caramelize the sugar.

Top with fresh fruit and serve immediately.

Makes 8 servings

*Baking time will vary slightly based on the depth of your crème brûlée dish.

Ice Cream

Caramel Ice Cream

7 ounces sugar

1 vanilla bean

4 cups milk

3/4 teaspoon salt

3/4 cup egg yolks

2 cups heavy cream

1 teaspoon vanilla extract

Slowly melt the sugar in a large saucepan over medium heat until golden amber, being careful not to let it burn. Stir occasionally until all of the sugar is melted.

With a sharp knife, split the vanilla bean down the center, scrape out its contents, and combine with the milk. Carefully add the milk to the sugar, and cook until the sugar is dissolved. Season with salt, and slowly temper in the egg yolks. Lower the heat and continue to whisk until the mixture thickens slightly. Strain through a chinois, and add the heavy cream and vanilla extract. Refrigerate until cold.

Spin the mixture in an ice cream machine according to the manufacturer's directions.

Makes 2 quarts

From caramel to cinnamon toast crunch, ice cream at Orchids is a celebration of our favorite childhood flavors. The combinations are really endless—but as with all recipes, it's best to stick with fresh ingredients.

Chocolate Ice Cream

1 1/2 cups milk

6 ounces sugar

1 1/2 cups heavy cream

6 egg yolks

4 ounces 64% dark chocolate, finely chopped

1 teaspoon vanilla extract

In a pot, bring the milk, sugar, and heavy cream to a boil. In a mixing bowl, whisk the egg yolks until light in color. Slowly temper in the milk mixture. Place the mixing bowl over a water bath, and cook until the mixture coats the back of a spoon.

Add the finely chopped chocolate and vanilla extract. Whisk until smooth. Strain through a chinois and cool in the refrigerator.

Spin the mixture in an ice cream machine according to the manufacturer's directions.

Makes 1 quart

Cinnamon Toast Crunch Ice Cream

2 cups milk

2 cinnamon sticks

1/2 vanilla bean

2 star anise

5 slices brioche, crust removed

1/2 cup unsalted butter, melted

4 ounces brown sugar

1/2 teaspoon ground cinnamon

7 egg yolks

1 cup sugar

1 teaspoon molasses

1 cup heavy cream

Preheat the oven to 350 degrees.

In a saucepan, bring the milk, cinnamon, vanilla bean, and star anise to a boil. Turn off the heat and steep for 30 minutes.

Meanwhile, dice the bread into 1/4-inch cubes and transfer to a mixing bowl.

Combine the melted butter, brown sugar, and cinnamon. Drizzle over the bread cubes.

Bake for 10-15 minutes until crispy and golden brown. Add half the cubes to the saucepan of milk and return to a boil. Remove from heat.

In a mixing bowl, whisk the egg yolks, sugar, and molasses. Slowly temper in the warm milk mixture. Return the liquid to a pot and heat to 185 degrees. Cook until thick enough to coat the back of a spoon. Remove from heat and strain into a mixing bowl. Add 1 cup of heavy cream.

Spin the mixture in an ice cream machine according to the manufacturer's directions. Fold in the remaining bread cubes.

Makes 2 quarts

White Peach Ice Cream

2 cups milk

6 ounces sugar

1 cup heavy cream

6 egg yolks

1 teaspoon vanilla extract

4 peeled and diced white peaches

Salt, to taste

In a pot, bring the milk, sugar, and heavy cream to a boil. In a mixing bowl, whisk the egg yolks until light in color. Slowly temper in the milk mixture. Place the mixing bowl over a water bath, and stir until the mixture coats the back of a spoon. Add the vanilla extract, white peaches, and salt. Cool in the refrigerator.

Spin in an ice cream machine according to the manufacturer's directions.

Makes 1 quart

Duet of Lemon Soufflé

FROZEN LEMON SOUFFLÉ

1/4 pound unsalted butter

1/4 cup plus 1 1/4 cups sugar

2 1/4 cups all-purpose flour

1/2 teaspoon vanilla extract

1 cup water

3 tablespoons cornstarch

10 tablespoons lemon juice

1 gelatin sheet, bloomed in cold water

2 egg whites

1 cup heavy cream

HOT SOUFFLÉ

3 tablespoons unsalted butter

3 tablespoons all-purpose flour

3/4 cup milk

1/4 cup Meyer lemon juice

1/2 cup sugar, plus extra for dusting

1 teaspoon vanilla extract

6 eggs

1 lemon, zested

1 teaspoon kosher salt

1 tablespoon unsalted butter, to coat

FOR THE FROZEN SOUFFLÉ: Preheat the oven to 350 degrees.

Combine the butter, 1/4 cup sugar, flour, and vanilla extract in a mixing bowl, and mix until a dough forms. Roll the dough into a thin layer on parchment paper, and bake for 10 minutes or until golden. Cool to room temperature. Pulse in a food processor until it breaks down.

In a saucepan, combine 1 1/4 cups sugar, water, cornstarch, and lemon juice. Cook over medium heat until thick. Remove from heat, add the gelatin, and whisk until completely dissolved. Transfer to the refrigerator and set for 4 hours.

In a stand-up mixer, whip the egg whites to stiff peaks. Fold the egg whites into the lemon mixture. Whip the cream to stiff peaks, and add to the lemon mixture.

Line the inside of 6 ring molds with acetate and transfer to a sheet tray. Press a layer of ground cake into the bottom of each ring mold. Divide the gelatin mixture over the top. Transfer to the freezer for 12 hours.

We love to serve soufflé two ways because it adds a lot of depth and variety to the plate. The first in this presentation is a frozen soufflé, edged with lemon and designed to refresh and cleanse the palate. The second is also lemon-scented—but is served warm after rising and puffing up in the oven.

FOR THE HOT SOUFFLÉ: Preheat the oven to 400 degrees.

Melt the butter in a small pot and add the flour. Stir to combine, and cook over low heat for 2 minutes. Pour in the milk, and continue to cook until the mixture is thick and pulls away from the sides of the pot. Add the lemon juice and sugar. Cook for 3 minutes more. Remove the pot from heat and add the vanilla.

Recipe and ingredients continued on page 154.

LEMON CURD

4 eggs

1 cup sugar

3/4 cup lemon juice

9 ounces unsalted butter, softened

CANDIED LEMONS

1 lemon

1 cup sugar

1 cup water

2 cardamom pods

Separate the eggs. Incorporate 4 yolks into the batter, one at a time, reserving 2 for another use. Fold in the lemon zest and salt.

Whip all the egg whites to soft peaks. Fold one third of the egg whites into the batter and incorporate. Fold in the remaining whites.

Thoroughly butter the inside of six 4-ounce soufflé cups. Dust the cups with sugar, shaking out the excess. Wipe off the rims to ensure that the soufflés rise evenly. Pour the soufflé batter into each cup. Bake for 20 minutes or until the batter rises 3 inches over the rim.

FOR THE LEMON CURD: Whisk the eggs and sugar in a bowl. Heat the lemon juice in a saucepan, and temper into the egg mixture. Cook over a water bath until 185 degrees and thick. Whisk in the butter, 1 tablespoon at a time. Chill in the refrigerator.

FOR THE CANDIED LEMONS: Slice the lemon and remove the seeds. Bring the sugar, water, and cardamom to a boil in a small pot. Reduce to a simmer and add the lemon slices. Poach for 10 minutes or until translucent.

TO SERVE: Carefully unmold the frozen soufflés. Place the frozen soufflés and the hot soufflé cups in the center of each serving plate. Garnish with lemon curd and candied lemons.

Makes 6 servings

Pineapple Upside Down Cake with Almond Streusel and Coconut

PINEAPPLE UPSIDE DOWN CAKES

Unsalted butter, to coat

1 cup plus 1 tablespoon all-purpose flour

1/2 teaspoon baking soda

1 teaspoon salt

3/4 cup sugar

1/2 cup unsalted butter

1 egg

1/2 teaspoon vanilla extract

6 tablespoons milk

1/2 lemon, zested and juiced

1/2 cup diced fresh pineapple

1/4 pineapple, sliced into 8 pieces

1 tablespoon brown sugar

ALMOND STREUSEL

1/4 cup all-purpose flour

1/4 cup almond flour

4 tablespoons unsalted butter

1/4 cup sugar

1 teaspoon Chinese five-spice

COCONUT GEL

3 3/4 cups coconut milk

5 ounces sugar

1 tablespoon kosher salt

1 tablespoon lemon zest

3/4 ounce agar powder

1 cup freshly squeezed lemon juice

8 thin slices pineapple

2 dozen fresh cherries

FOR THE PINEAPPLE UPSIDE DOWN CAKES: Preheat the oven to 350 degrees. Grease eight 4-ounce ramekins with butter and set aside.

Sift the flour, baking soda, and salt into a mixing bowl.

In a separate mixing bowl, cream the sugar and butter until light and fluffy. Add the egg and vanilla extract and mix well.

Add half the dry ingredients to the butter mixture. Pour in the milk and mix again. Add the other half of the dry ingredients and the lemon juice, zest, and diced pineapple. Mix well.

Place a pineapple slice in the bottom of each ramekin. Sprinkle with brown sugar.

Fill the ramekins two-thirds of the way with batter and bake for 40 minutes. Store at room temperature.

FOR THE ALMOND STREUSEL: Blend all the ingredients in a food processor. Transfer to a sheet tray, and bake at 350 degrees for 5 minutes or until lightly toasted.

FOR THE COCONUT GEL: In a saucepan, bring the coconut milk, sugar, salt, and lemon zest to a boil. Remove from heat and steep for 20 minutes. Strain and return the liquid to the saucepan. Add the agar powder and bring to a boil. Cook for 2 minutes and strain onto a plastic-lined sheet pan. Cool in the refrigerator.

When the mixture is set, transfer to a blender and add the lemon juice. Blend on high until well incorporated. Return to refrigerator until needed.

TO SERVE: Warm the cakes in the oven. Flip the ramekins onto each serving plate, and garnish with coconut gel, almond streusel, curled pineapple slices, and cherries.

Makes 8 servings

As a kid, I spent a few years living on an island off the coast of Africa. The locals would cut pineapples off the trees and dip them in the ocean after they cut off the skin. I thought they were cleaning them at first—until I realized they were actually seasoning the fruit with saltwater. It was a cooking lesson I never forgot: even the smallest amount of salt brings out the natural sweetness in nearly everything.

Frozen Crèmesicle Semifreddo with Almond Tuile

CRÈMESICLE SEMIFREDDO

3 eggs, plus 2 egg yolks
3 ounces granulated sugar
2 oranges, juiced and zested
1 vanilla bean, split and scraped
1/4 cup Cointreau
2 ounces heavy cream
6 ounces crème fraîche (pg 168)

ALMOND TUILE

1/2 pound unsalted butter
1/2 pound sugar
3/4 cup sliced almonds
2 ounces white sesame seeds
2 ounces black sesame seeds
1/2 teaspoon ground cardamom
1 ounce bread flour
2 ounces milk
1 ounce corn syrup

ICE WINE REDUCTION

2 cups red ice wine
1 cup sugar
1 tablespoon cloves
1/2 cup scraped vanilla bean

CANDIED CURRANTS

1 cup red currants
1/2 cup granulated sugar

CANDIED ORANGE ZEST

1 cup sugar
3/4 cup water
4 oranges, zested and julienned

FOR THE SEMIFREDDO: Use acetate to line the inside of 8 ring molds.

Whisk together the eggs, yolks, sugar, orange zest, and vanilla bean over a water bath until the sugar is dissolved and the mixture reaches 120 degrees. Transfer to a stand-up mixer with a whisk attachment. Whip until light and fluffy; the mixture should be room temperature and form a ribbon when dropped from a spoon. Fold in the Cointreau and orange juice. Reserve.

Whip the heavy cream and crème fraîche to medium-soft peaks in a stand-up mixer. Fold the crème fraîche into the egg mixture.

Transfer the mousse to a pastry bag, and pipe into the ring molds. Freeze overnight before unmolding and removing the acetate.

FOR THE TUILE: Preheat the oven to 350 degrees.

Mix the tuile ingredients in a bowl and refrigerate. Once thoroughly chilled, roll the dough between 2 pieces of parchment paper into a 1/4-inch-thick layer. Remove the top piece of parchment paper and transfer to an inverted baking sheet. Bake for 10 minutes or until golden brown.

While the tuile is still hot, cut out 8 pieces equal to the circumference of the frozen soufflés and 2 inches shorter. Wrap each tuile around the ring mold until set, then wrap around the base of the frozen soufflés.

FOR THE ICE WINE REDUCTION: Combine all the ingredients in a sauce pot and bring to a boil. Stir until the sugar is dissolved. Cook until reduced by half and the mixture has thickened to a syrup consistency. Strain the sauce and set aside.

FOR THE CANDIED CURRANTS: Freeze the currants, roll in sugar, and store in the freezer until ready to use.

FOR THE CANDIED ORANGE ZEST: Combine the sugar and water in a small pot and bring to a boil. Add the zest and cook until translucent. Store the zest in the cooking liquid until ready to use.

TO SERVE: Place a semifreddo on each plate. Garnish with a drizzle of ice wine reduction, candied currants, and candied orange zest.

Makes 8 servings

This dessert is special because it's bright and refreshing—and because of the unique preparation involved. While the almond tuiles are still warm from the oven, we bend them into perfect rings, let them set, and then wrap them around the frozen soufflés.

Mignardise

French Macarons

MACARONS

4 ounces almond flour

8 ounces powdered sugar

4 ounces egg whites

2 ounces sugar

ORANGE BUTTERCREAM FILLING

4 egg whites

1 cup sugar

8 ounces unsalted butter

1/3 cup Cointreau

1 tablespoon orange zest

Preheat the oven to 350 degrees.

Blend the almond flour and powdered sugar in a food processor to a fine powder. Sift into a mixing bowl.

In another mixing bowl, whip the egg whites to soft peaks and add the sugar. Continue to whip to stiff peaks.

Fold the almond mixture into the egg whites, and transfer to a piping bag fitted with a round tip. Pipe a series of 1-inch circles onto several parchment-lined sheet pans.

Transfer the sheet pans to the oven, and bake for 7-10 minutes or until the macarons are light brown and slightly crispy.

Mignardise are complimentary petit fours served at the end of the meal, and their variations are endless. Whether the daily selection includes chocolate buckeyes filled with peanut butter, an assortment of seasonal pâte de fruits, or crunchy French macarons, they're a sweet gift to our diners—a final touch at the end of the meal.

FOR THE ORANGE BUTTERCREAM: In a metal mixing bowl, combine the egg whites and sugar. Whisk over a water bath until the sugar is dissolved and the mixture reaches 160 degrees.

Transfer to a stand-up mixer fitted with a whip attachment. Beat until the mixture forms thick, glossy peaks and has come to room temperature.

With the mixer still running, add the butter, 1 tablespoon at a time, making sure each addition is completely incorporated before adding the next. Add the Cointreau and orange zest. Mix until smooth.

Sandwich the orange buttercream between two macarons using a piping bag.

Pâte de Fruits

18 ounces fruit purée, apple, apricot, or raspberry

1 ounce glucose

1 ounce pectin

26 ounces sugar, plus extra for dusting

1 teaspoon citric acid

Combine the fruit purée and glucose in a small pot and bring to a boil. Combine the pectin and 2 ounces of sugar, and add to the pot. Bring the mixture to a boil again and add the remaining sugar.

Bring the liquid to 225 degrees over medium-high heat, whisking constantly. Add the citric acid. Pour the mixture onto a parchment-lined half sheet pan. Set at room temperature. Cut the pâte de fruits into desired shapes and dust with sugar.

Chocolate Truffles

Variation 1
GANACHE TRUFFLE FILLING

6 ounces heavy cream

8 ounces Valrhona, Manjari 64% chocolate, finely chopped

4 ounces unsalted butter, softened

Variation 2
BUCKEYE TRUFFLE FILLING

2 ounces unsalted butter, softened

4 ounces peanut butter

3 ounces powdered sugar

1/2 ounce dark rum

TRUFFLE CHOCOLATE

16 ounces tempered chocolate

FOR THE GANACHE FILLING: Bring the heavy cream to a boil, and pour into a bowl with the chocolate. Allow the heat of the cream to melt the chocolate and whisk. Once the mixture is cooled to room temperature, whisk in the softened butter.

FOR THE BUCKEYE FILLING: In a mixing bowl, combine the softened butter, peanut butter, powdered sugar, and dark rum. Whip until light and fluffy.

TO COMPLETE: Pour a small amount of the tempered chocolate into a tray of candy molds. Swirl to coat, and pour out the excess. Allow the chocolate in the molds to set at room temperature.

Fill the molds with either ganache filling (variation 1) or buckeye filling (variation 2). Pour in a sealing coating of tempered chocolate, scraping off any excess with a knife. Set the chocolates at room temperature before unmolding.

PANTRY

Tomato Water

4 diced ripe tomatoes
2 tablespoons kosher salt

Purée the tomatoes and salt in a food processor for 1 minute. Position a chinois lined with cheesecloth over a bain-marie or mixing bowl. Pour in the puréed tomatoes and strain. Transfer the chinois and bowl to the refrigerator, and continue to strain overnight, being careful not to agitate the liquid.

Tomato water lasts for 1 week refrigerated in an airtight container.

Makes 1 cup

Tomato Concassé

Tomatoes, as needed

Carve a shallow "x" in the bottom of each tomato and plunge into a pot of boiling water. After 10 seconds, transfer the tomatoes to an ice bath to stop the cooking process. Gently remove the skins and discard. Quarter each tomato, and cut out the pulp and seeds. Dice each quarter into 1/4-inch cubes.

Lemon Vinaigrette

1/4 cup freshly squeezed lemon juice
1/2 cup extra virgin olive oil
1 teaspoon kosher salt

Combine all the ingredients.

Makes 1 cup

Soy Gelée

1/4 cup soy sauce
1 3/4 cups chicken stock (pg 166)
1/2 tablespoon black vinegar
1-inch piece minced ginger
1/4 minced jalapeño, seeds removed
1 minced scallion
2 teaspoons agar powder
3 sheets gelatin, soaked
in cold water until soft

In a sauce pot, bring the soy sauce, chicken stock, vinegar, ginger, jalapeño, and scallions to a simmer. Remove from heat and allow the mixture to steep for 15 minutes. Strain into another pot and discard the solids. Add the agar and bring to a boil, then reduce to a simmer for 2 minutes. Whisk in the gelatin and mix until dissolved. Pour the liquid into a shallow container lined with plastic wrap. Refrigerate overnight, then dice into 1/4-inch pieces.

Soy gelée lasts for 1 week refrigerated in an airtight container.

Makes 2 cups

Coriander Oil

1/4 cup coriander seeds
2 cups vegetable oil

In a sauté pan, toast the coriander seeds over low heat for 2 minutes or until fragrant. Add the vegetable oil and bring the temperature to 150 degrees. Cool the liquid to room temperature and then reheat to 150 degrees. Steep the coriander in the oil overnight.

Place the coriander and oil in a blender and purée on high for 5 minutes. Strain through a coffee filter and reserve.

Coriander oil lasts for 1 week refrigerated in an airtight container.

Makes 2 cups

Curry Oil

2 minced shallots
7 ounces grape seed oil
6 tablespoons curry powder
2 ounces water

Sauté the shallots in 1 tablespoon of oil, and cook slowly until tender. Add the curry powder, and cook for 2 minutes or until fragrant. Add the water, and cook until completely evaporated. Pour in the remaining oil, and steep at room temperature for 6 hours. Refrigerate and strain through a coffee filter.

Makes 1 cup

Preserved Lemons

10 lemons

2 tablespoons black peppercorns

1 tablespoon coriander seeds

1 tablespoon fennel seeds

1 cup kosher salt

3 star anise

2 bay leaves

1 tablespoon saffron

3 cups extra virgin olive oil

Cut each lemon from top to bottom, making a vertical incision about a 1/2-inch deep, but not cutting all the way through. Make a horizontal slit from left to right, forming a shallow "x." In a small bowl, squeeze out the lemon juice and set aside.

In a sauté pan, toast the peppercorns, coriander, and fennel until fragrant, about 1 minute. Add to a small bowl with three-fourths of the salt and the star anise, bay leaves, and saffron. Season the inside of the lemons with this mixture and place them slit-side-up in a plastic container. Cover with reserved lemon juice and olive oil. Sprinkle with the remaining salt.

Store in the refrigerator for 6 weeks or until the lemons are soft to the touch. Remove the skins with a sharp paring knife.

Preserved lemons can be refrigerated almost indefinitely in an airtight container.

Makes 10 preserved lemons

Chicken Stock

5 pounds chicken backs

1 chopped onion

1 chopped carrot

3 chopped celery ribs

3 thyme sprigs

1/2 tablespoon black peppercorns

1 bay leaf

Rinse the bones until the water runs clear. Transfer to a large stockpot and cover with 3 inches of cold water. Place over high heat, and as the water begins to simmer, skim off any impurities that rise to the top. When the water begins to boil, turn off the heat and discard the water.

Rinse the bones thoroughly under cold running water, and return them to the stockpot. Add enough water to cover by 3 inches once more, and add in the remaining ingredients. Simmer for 12 hours, skimming the surface every 30 minutes to remove impurities. Strain and discard the bones.

Chicken stock can be stored in an airtight container for several months or frozen almost indefinitely.

Makes 1 gallon

Veal Stock

10 pounds veal knuckle bones
1 pound diced carrots
1 pound diced celery ribs
2 pounds diced onion
1 cup tomato paste
6 thyme sprigs
3 tablespoons black peppercorns
3 bay leaves

Preheat the oven to 400 degrees.

Rinse the bones until the water runs clear. Transfer to a large stockpot, and cover with 3 inches of cold water. Apply high heat, and as the water begins to simmer, skim off any impurities that rise to the top. When the water begins to boil, turn off the heat and discard the water.

Repeat this process two more times, covering the bones with 3 inches of water, skimming off impurities, and straining and discarding the liquid. Place the bones back in the stockpot, and cover once more with water.

Place the carrots, celery, and onions on a sheet tray, and roast in the oven until caramelized. Coat the vegetables in tomato paste and return to the oven for 5 minutes.

Transfer the vegetable mixture to the stockpot and add the thyme, peppercorns, and bay leaves. Bring the liquid to a simmer and cook for 18 hours, skimming off impurities every 30 minutes. Strain the stock and cool.

Veal stock can be stored in an airtight container for several months or frozen almost indefinitely.

Makes 1 gallon

Roasted Garlic

5 garlic heads
3 tablespoons extra virgin olive oil
1 tablespoon kosher salt

Preheat the oven to 350 degrees.

With a sharp knife, cut off the root ends of the heads of garlic, about a 1/2 inch from the bottom. Transfer to a baking dish and toss with the olive oil and salt. Cover the dish with foil, and bake for 45 minutes or until the garlic is tender. Using the back of your knife, squeeze the garlic out of its skin.

If not using immediately, cover the garlic with olive oil and store in the refrigerator for up to 1 week.

Makes approximately 50 roasted garlic cloves

Crème Fraîche

1 cup 36% fat heavy cream
2 tablespoons buttermilk

In a non-reactive bowl, combine the cream and buttermilk. Cover with plastic wrap and store in a warm place, preferably 80 degrees. After 12 hours, check the consistency—variations in temperature will speed up or slow down the thickening process.

Makes 1 cup

Satsuma Mandarin Orange Miso Aioli

2 cups Satsuma mandarin orange juice
1/4 cup white miso
1/4 teaspoon minced garlic
1 teaspoon minced ginger
3/4 cup mayonnaise
1 teaspoon lime juice
1 1/2 tablespoons rice wine vinegar
1 1/2 teaspoons sesame oil

In a sauce pot, reduce the orange juice to 1/4 cup over high heat. Transfer to a blender and add the remaining ingredients. Mix on high until well incorporated.

Satsuma mandarin orange miso aioli can be refrigerated in an airtight container for up to 1 week.

Makes 3 cups

Purple Potato Chips

1 purple potato
Vegetable oil, for frying
Kosher salt, to taste

Slice the potato and rinse under cold water.

Pour vegetable oil into a large, heavy pot or deep-fryer and heat to 350 degrees. Fry the potatoes until crispy. Salt to taste, and drain on a paper towel.

Makes 1 serving

Roasted Red Peppers

4 red bell peppers
2 tablespoons extra virgin olive oil
1 tablespoon sea salt

Preheat the oven to 350 degrees.

In a mixing bowl, toss the peppers in the olive oil and sea salt. Transfer to a sheet tray, and roast the peppers until their skins start to blister. Place the peppers back in the mixing bowl and cover with plastic wrap. When cool enough to handle, use a paring knife to gently remove the skins. Split the peppers with a knife and remove the seeds.

Parsley Oil

1 quart Italian parsley leaves, stems discarded
1 cup extra virgin olive oil
Kosher salt, to taste

In a medium pot, blanch the parsley in boiling, salted water for 10 seconds. Transfer to an ice bath to stop further cooking. Squeeze the parsley, removing as much water as possible. Transfer to a blender and mix on high, drizzling in olive oil until the mixture is the consistency of wet sand. Season to taste with salt. Line a chinois, and strain the parsley in the refrigerator for 3 hours. Discard the parsley and reserve the parsley oil in a squeeze bottle.

Makes 1 cup

INDEX

Seared Foie Gras with Concord Grapes, Vanilla Pound Cake, and Poached Quince, 44

Eggplant
Crispy Artisanal Feta Cheese with Katafi, Heirloom Eggplant, Harissa, and Herbed Crème Fraîche, 22

Eggplant Timbale with Olive Oil Emulsion, Crispy Fennel, and Roasted Tomatoes, 96

Minestrone with White Beans, Ricotta Tortellini, and Crispy Serrano Ham, 53

Eggs
Maine Lobster Salad with "Crispy" Poached Egg, Parsley, and Domestic Caviar Cream, 30

Saffron Cauliflower Custard with House-Smoked Bacon, Domestic Caviar, and Crème Fraîche, 16

Seared Scallops with Sweet Corn, Baby Carrots, Crispy Mirin-Glazed Pork Belly, Quail Eggs, Almonds, and Curry Oil, 81

Endive
Blue Cheese Beignets with Local Honey, Frisée, Belgian Endive, and Almond Brittle, 64

Fava Beans *See Beans*

Fennel
Eggplant Timbale with Olive Oil Emulsion, Crispy Fennel, and Roasted Tomatoes, 96

Floating Mozzarella with 3-Hour Tomatoes, Roasted Fennel, Lavash, and Tomato Water Gelée, 18

Shrimp Cavatelli with Tomato Concassé, Braised Fennel, and Clam Nage, 36

Feta
Crispy Artisanal Feta Cheese with Katafi, Heirloom Eggplant, Harissa, and Herbed Crème Fraîche, 22

Feuilletine
Chocolate Bavarian with Milk Chocolate Biscuit and Marinated Blackberries, 139

Figs
Mâche Salad with Port Wine Yuzu Vinaigrette, Brie and Fig Grilled Cheese, and Candied Huckleberries, 70

Old Kentucky Tomme with Bourbon Barrel Vanilla Sorghum, Lavash, and Honeycomb, 144

Fish and Shellfish *See also Clams; Crab; Halibut; Lobster; Loup de Mer; Monkfish; Oysters; Salmon; Scallops; Shrimp; Skate; Snapper; Tuna*

Crab Bisque with Basmati Rice, Salt and Pepper Crab, and Rice Cracker, 56

Duet of Tuna with Lychees, Pickled Shiitake Mushrooms, Sprouts, and Satsuma Mandarin Orange Miso Aioli, 27

Gulf Snapper "en Papillote" with Vidalia Onions, Curry Vinaigrette, and Green Apple Tzatziki, 78

Halibut Cheeks with Green Garlic Gnudi, Wild Asparagus, and Truffle Vinaigrette, 100

Loup de Mer with Bay Scallops, Sage, Golden Raisins, Orange Reduction, and Caramelized Cauliflower, 102

Maine Lobster Salad with "Crispy" Poached Egg, Parsley, and Domestic Caviar Cream, 30

Monkfish Paillard with Smoked Bacon, Lime, Cashews, and Arugula, 92

Oyster Velouté with Sweetbreads, Tapioca Pearls, and Kusshi Oysters, 60

Poached Halibut with Sunchokes, Haricots Verts, Dungeness Crab, and Tarragon, 84

Potato-Wrapped Salmon with Ham Hock Broth, Cipollini Onions, Dried Cherries, and Lovage, 86

Seared Scallops with Sweet Corn, Baby Carrots, Crispy Mirin-Glazed Pork Belly, Quail Eggs, Almonds, and Curry Oil, 81

Seared Truffle-Marinated Tuna with Wilted Brussels Sprouts, Smoked Bacon, Soy Gelée, and Worcestershire Aioli, 76

Shrimp Cavatelli with Tomato Concassé, Braised Fennel, and Clam Nage, 36

Skate Wing with Brown Butter Nage, Artichokes, Grilled Porcini, Capers, and Golden Raisins, 89

Smoked Salmon with Red Onion Marmalade, Crème Fraîche, and Potato Crisp, 42

Tuna Tartare with Watermelon Radishes, Cucumber Water, and Lemon Oil, 32

Yellowtail Snapper with Littleneck Clams, Braised Leeks, and Parsley Vinaigrette, 94

Flan *See Custard*

Flowers
English Pea Purée with Fava Beans, White and Green Asparagus, Tarragon, and Parmesan Cheese, 72

Mâche Salad with Port Wine Yuzu Vinaigrette, Brie and Fig Grilled Cheese, and Candied Huckleberries, 70

Roasted Quail with Spiced Pumpkin Purée, Pepitas, Pomegranates, and Port Wine Hibiscus Reduction, 129

Foie Gras *See Duck*

Frisée
Blue Cheese Beignets with Local Honey, Frisée, Belgian Endive, and Almond Brittle, 64

Veal Sweetbreads with Celery Salad, Haricots Verts, Shiitake Mushrooms, and Smoked Paprika Vinaigrette, 39

Fruit *See also specific fruits*
Crème Brûlée with Seasonal Fruit, 146

Pâte de Fruit, 162

Galette
Beef Shabu-Shabu with Vermicelli Galette and Dried Mushroom Broth, 48

Rabbit with Serrano Ham, Foie Gras, Polenta Galette, White Asparagus, and Raspberries, 121

Game *See Rabbit; Venison*

Game Birds *See Duck, Quail*

Ganache *See also Chocolate*
Chocolate Decadence, 142

Chocolate Truffles, 162

Garlic
Grilled Ramp Tortellini with Morel Mushrooms, Arugula, and Roasted Garlic Butter Sauce, 67

Halibut Cheeks with Green Garlic Gnudi, Wild Asparagus, and Truffle Vinaigrette, 100

Roasted Garlic, 167

Shrimp Cavatelli with Tomato Concassé, Braised Fennel, and Clam Nage, 36

Gelée
Beef Shabu-Shabu with Vermicelli Galette and Dried Mushroom Broth, 48

Floating Mozzarella with 3-Hour Tomatoes, Roasted Fennel, Lavash, and Tomato Water Gelée, 18

Seared Truffle-Marinated Tuna with Wilted Brussels Sprouts, Smoked Bacon, Soy Gelée, and Worcestershire Aioli, 76

Soy Gelée, 165

Ginger
Roasted Lamb Loin with Carrot Ginger Purée, Matignon, Lemon Churro, and Madeira Sauce, 118

Gnudi
Braised Beef Cheeks with Spinach Gnudi, Shimeji Mushrooms, and Roasted Tomatoes, 111

Halibut Cheeks with Green Garlic Gnudi, Wild Asparagus, and Truffle Vinaigrette, 100

Gold Leaves
Chocolate Decadence, 142

Graham Crackers
S'mores with Warm Chocolate Custard, 136

Grapefruit
Crispy Tofu with Smoked Paprika, Arugula, and Grapefruit, 106

Grapes
Crème Brûlée with Seasonal Fruit, 146

Seared Foie Gras with Concord Grapes, Vanilla Pound Cake, and Poached Quince, 44

Gratinée
Grilled Filet Mignon with Oyster Mushroom Gratinée, 132

Green Beans *See Haricots Verts*

Gruyére
Eggplant Timbale with Olive Oil Emulsion, Crispy Fennel, and Roasted Tomatoes, 96

Grilled Filet Mignon with Oyster Mushroom Gratinée, 132

Halibut
Halibut Cheeks with Green Garlic Gnudi, Wild Asparagus, and Truffle Vinaigrette, 100

Poached Halibut with Sunchokes, Haricots Verts, Dungeness Crab, and Tarragon, 84

Ham
Minestrone with White Beans, Ricotta Tortellini, and Crispy Serrano Ham, 53

Potato-Wrapped Salmon with Ham Hock Broth, Cipollini Onions, Dried Cherries, and Lovage, 86

Rabbit with Serrano Ham, Foie Gras, Polenta Galette, White Asparagus, and Raspberries, 121

Haricots Verts
Poached Halibut with Sunchokes, Haricots Verts, Dungeness Crab, and Tarragon, 84

Veal Sweetbreads with Celery Salad, Haricots Verts, Shiitake Mushrooms, and Smoked Paprika Vinaigrette, 39

Harissa
Crispy Artisanal Feta Cheese with Katafi, Heirloom Eggplant, Harissa, and Herbed Crème Fraîche, 22